Katherine Anne Porter's Fiction

*I can't tell you what gives true intensity,
but I know it when I find it, even in my own work—
there perhaps first of all. It is not a matter of
how you feel, at any one moment, certainly not at
the moment of writing. A calculated coldness is the
best mood for that, most often. Feeling is more
than mood, it is a whole way of being, it is the
nature you are born with, you cannot invent it. The
question is, how to convey a sense of whatever is
there, as feeling, within you, to the reader; and
that is a problem of technical expertness.*

*From the journal of
Katherine Anne Porter*

Katherine Anne Porter's Fiction

by M. M. Liberman

Wayne State University Press   Detroit, 1971

Permissions
"Ship of Fools and the Critics," by Theodore Solotaroff.
Reprinted from Commentary, by permission; copyright
© 1962 by the American Jewish Committee.
Wayne Booth "Yes, But Are They Really Novels"
(review), in The Yale Review, copyright Yale
University Press.
"A Country and Some People I Love," in Harper's
September 1965. Copyright © 1965 by Katherine Anne
Porter.
"Notes on Writing," in New Directions in Prose and
Poetry, 1940. Copyright © 1941 by Katherine Anne
Porter; copyright renewed 1969. Reprinted by permission
of the author.
"Some Observations on the Genesis of Ships of Fools: A
Letter from Katherine Anne Porter." Reprinted by
permission of the Modern Language Association of
America from PMLA 84 (1969).
For permission to quote from "María Concepción" and
"The Leaning Tower" acknowledgment is made to
Harcourt, Brace, Jovanovich, Inc. to reprint excerpts
from The Collected Stories of Katherine Anne Porter,
copyright, 1930, 1935, 1936, 1941, 1958, 1963, 1964, by
Katherine Anne Porter.
From Introduction by Allan Tate to the Signet Classic
edition of Sanctuary by William Faulkner. Copyright ©
1968 by the New American Library, Inc. By permission
of the New American Library, Inc., New York and the
author.
"A Wreath for the Gamekeeper," in Encounter, vol. 14,
February 1960. Copyright © 1960 by Katherine Anne
Porter. Reprinted by permission of the author.
D. H. Lawrence, Lady Chatterley's Lover. Published by
Grove Press, Inc.
Quotations from "Holiday" and Encounter, copyright ©
1960 by Katherine Anne Porter. Reprinted by
permission of Cyrilly Abels.

Contents

Acknowledgments

I am indebted for their cooperation to the staffs of the Burling, Houghton, and Newberry libraries and to the libraries of the University of Iowa and the University of Texas; to Professors Edward E. Foster and Sheldon P. Zitner for reading portions of this book in manuscript and offering valuable suggestions. For grant assistance, I am grateful to the Newberry Library and to Grinnell College. Thanks are due Miss Loretta Smith and Mrs. Carol Mergen for invaluable secretarial help, and to Miss Gail Gilman, and especially to Mrs. Marguerite Wallace for the employment of their highly professional editorial talents. To Miss Katherine Anne Porter and to her attorney, E. Barrett Prettyman, Jr., I am grateful for permission to make use of heretofore unpublished materials.

M. M. Liberman

Preface

The exceptionally high quality of the fiction of Katherine Anne Porter is not to be accounted for entirely by historical-biographical means, by an exclusive attention to her serious and universal themes, or by an analysis of her striking use of mythic material alone. It is, to be accounted for also, and in great measure, by its formal properties, verbal and rhetorical. Those make clear an impressive talent for showing forth a first-rate and peculiarly feminine intelligence in a compositional mode precisely appropriate to its singular feeling.

Miss Porter's fictional means are traditional and conventional in the best sense of those terms, as befits a classical modern artist.

My hope is that by a study of Miss Porter's evident methods and apparent intentions, as they are discernible in her most problematical or engaging works—there is none extant—to make some modest contribution to enhancing, if not rescuing, the reputation of a splendid writer.

Classic I employ in Arnold's judicial sense to mean "the class of the very best," to a lesser degree in the historical sense of deriving by tradition from the monumental models, and to a considerable degree in the formal sense, in contrast to *romantic,* to mean an elevation, as principles of composition, of reason and control over emotionality and spontaneity.

Since I was introduced to it many years ago, I have admired Percy Lubbock's *The Craft of Fiction,* and I have had in mind that kind of work, among others, insofar as I have consciously treated of Miss Porter's work, as Lubbock did of James's and Flaubert's, both to pay her tribute and to illustrate some theoretical claims.

Chapter I
The Responsibility of the Novelist and the Critical Reception of Ship of Fools

I

The title of this chapter is deliberately somewhat misleading, in the way that a title can be when it seems to promise a discourse on an arguable concept. In this instance, it suggests a certain premise, namely, that the question, What does the author owe society? is one which still lives and breathes. In fact, I think this question no longer does. I suspect, rather, that its grave can be located somewhere between two contentions: André Gide's, that the artist is under no moral obligation to present a useful idea, but that he is under a moral obligation to present an idea well; and Henry James's, that we are being arbitrary if we demand, to begin with, more of a novel than that it be interesting. As James uses the word *novel* here, I take it to mean any extended, largely realistic, narrative fiction, but his view is applicable as well to fiction in other forms and modes.

One might say that if a literary work is more than immediately engaging, if, for example, it stimulates the moral imagination, it is doing more than is fairly required of it as art.

Why, then, if I think it is in most respects dead, do I choose to raise the question of the writer's responsibility? The answer is that I do not choose to raise the question. The question is continually being raised for me and, because literature is my profession, it haunts my house. Thus, I am moved to invoke certain commonplaces, as in the above, of a sort I had supposed to be news only to very few. This was the case markedly on the occasion of the publication of Katherine Anne Porter's *Ship of Fools* in 1962. Twenty years in the making, a book club selection even before it was set up in type, restlessly awaited by a faithful coterie, reviewed widely and discussed broadly almost simultaneously with its appearance on the store shelves, this book caused and still causes consternation in the world of contemporary letters to a degree that I find interesting, curious, and suspect. The focus of this chapter will be on the critical reception of the book and I hope that the relevance of what remains of the responsibility question will issue naturally from it. I must, however, quote at awkward length, in two instances, in order to be fair to other commentators.

The first brief wave of reviews was almost unanimous in its praise of *Ship of Fools* and then very shortly the many dissenting opinions began to appear, usually in the most respectable intellectual journals where reviewers claim to be, and often are, critics. These reviews were characterized by one of two dominant feelings: bitter resentment or acute disappointment. A remarkable instance of the former appeared in the prestigious journal *Commentary* as its feature article of the month, under the byline of one of its associate editors. That Miss Porter's book should have been originally well received so rankled *Commentary*'s staff that a lengthy rebuttal was composed, taking priority over other articles on ordinarily more pressing subjects, such as impending nuclear destruction and race violence. The article progresses to a frothing vehemence in its later pages. I will quote from the opening of the piece which begins relatively calmly, as follows:

> Whatever the problems were that kept Katherine Anne Porter's *Ship of Fools* from appearing during the past twenty years, it has been leading a charmed life ever since it was published last March. In virtually a single voice, a little cracked and breathless with

excitement, the reviewers announced that Miss Porter's long-awaited first novel was a "triumph," a "masterpiece," a "work of genius . . . a momentous work of fiction," a "phenomenal, rich, and delectable book," a "literary event of the highest magnitude." Whether it was Mark Schorer in the *New York Times Book Review* delivering a lecture, both learned and lyrical, on the source, sensibility and stature of the novel ("Call it . . . the Middle-march of a later day"), or a daily reviewer for the San Francisco *Call Bulletin* confessing that "not once had he started a review with so much admiration for its author, . . ." in the end it came to the same thing.

Riding the crest of this wave of acclaim, *Ship of Fools* made its way to the top of the best-seller lists in record time and it is still there as I write in mid-September. During these four months, it has encountered virtually as little opposition in taking its place among the classics of literature as it did in taking and holding its place on the best-seller lists. A few critics . . . wound up by saying that *Ship of Fools* fell somewhat short of greatness with respectful seriousness. Some of the solid citizens among the reviewers, like John K. Hutchens, found the novel to be dull and said so. Here and there, mainly in the hinterlands, a handful of independent spirits . . . suspected that the book was a failure. But who was listening?

Prominent among the circumstances which have helped to make a run-away best-seller and a *succes d'estime* out of this massive, unexciting, and saturnine novel was the aura of interest, partly sentimental and partly deserved, that Miss Porter's long struggle with it had produced. Most of the reviews begin in the same way: a distinguished American short-story writer at the age of seventy-one has finally finished her first novel after twenty years of working on it. As this point was developed, it tended to establish the dominant tone of many reviews—that of an elated witness to a unique personal triumph, almost as though this indomitable septuagenarian had not written a book, but had done something even more remarkable—like swimming the English Channel.[1]

The *Commentary* critic goes on to charge Miss Porter with having written a novel contemptible in two decisive ways: (1) badly executed in every conceivable technical sense, particularly characterization, and (2) unacceptable on moral grounds, being pessimistic and misanthropic: "But the soul of humanity is lacking," he says, quoting still another reviewer sympathetic to his own position. Why Dostoevski, for example, is permitted to be both massive and saturnine and Miss Porter not is a question spoken to later only by implication. The critic's charge that her writing is "unexciting" is curious considering his own highly emotional state in responding to the work. The charge of misanthropy is, of course, directly related to the alleged technical failure of the characterization, which he says "borders on caricature" in the way it portrays nearly every human type as loathesome and grotesque, with hardly a single redeeming feature. In considering the charge of misanthropy we are, perforce, confronted with the question of the writer's social responsibility in the moral sphere, for the attribution of misanthropy to a writer by a critic is typically a censure and is seldom merely a description of the writer's stance. The writer is usually, as in this case, denied the right to be misanthropic on the ground that it is immoral to hate and, given the writer's influential function, it is deemed irresponsible of him to clothe such a negative sentiment as hate in intellectually attractive garb. In my efforts at synthesis, I will get back to these questions. But for the moment I will point out that *Commentary's* view of *Ship of Fools* as depicting mankind in a hatefully distorted, therefore untruthful, therefore immoral way, is in fact the view of the book commonly held by the normally intelligent and reasonably well-educated reader of fiction, if my impressions are accurate; these impressions are based, in small part, incidentally, on the way the book was received on college campuses, where it was in one instance required reading for freshmen in a week of panel discussions before the onset of formal instruction. The book was selected, I was told, because it was thought controversial and dealt with themes of human import. Scarcely anyone could stomach the book and the few who did, I understand, did not blush to inform the new students of its putative unfortunate characteristics.

I turn now to the other mode of reception: acute disappointment. One of the most clearly and intelligently presented discussions of this group was Wayne Booth's critique in the *Yale Review* from which I quote as follows:

> Katherine Ann Porter's long-awaited novel is more likely to fall afoul of one's bias for finely-constructed, concentrated plots. In this respect her own earlier fiction works against her; part of the strength of those classics, *Pale Horse, Pale Rider* and *Noon Wine,* lies in their concision, their economy, their simplicity. *There is my* Katherine Anne Porter, I am tempted to protest, as she offers me, now, something so different as to be almost unrecognizable—a 225,000-word novel (more words, I suppose, than in all of the rest of her works put together) with nearly fifty characters. What is worse, the manner of narration is fragmented, diluted. Her plan is to create a shipload of lost souls and to follow them, isolated moment by isolated moment, in their alienated selfishness, through the nasty, exasperating events of a twenty-seven day voyage, in 1931, from Veracruz to Bremerhaven. She deliberately avoids concentrating strongly on any one character; even the four or five that are granted some sympathy are kept firmly, almost allegorically, subordinated to the portrayal of the ship of fools ("I am a passenger on that ship," she reminds us in an opening note).

> Her method is sporadic, almost desultory, and her unity is based on theme and idea rather than coherence of action. We flash from group to group, scene to scene, mind to mind, seldom remaining with any group or observer for longer than three or four pages together. While the book is as a result full of crosslights and ironic juxtapositions, it has, for me, no steady center of interest except the progressively more intense exemplification of its central truth: men are pitifully, foolishly self-alienated. At the heart of man lies a radical corruption that can only occasionally, fitfully, be overcome by love. . . .

> Once the various groupings are established—the four isolated, self-torturing Americans, two of them lovers who hate and fear

each other when they are not loving; the sixteen Germans, most of them in self-destructive family groups, and all but two of them repugnant almost beyond comedy; the depraved swarm of Spanish dancers with their two demon-children; the carefree and viciously irresponsible Cuban students; the half-mad, lost Spanish countess; the morose Swede; and so on—each group or lone traveler is taken to some sort of climactic moment, more often in the form of a bungled chance for genuine human contact. These little anti-climaxes are scattered throughout the latter fourth of the book, but for most of the characters the nadir is reached during the long "gala" evening, almost at the end of the journey. . . . Such a work, lacking, by design, a grand causal, temporal sequence, depends for complete success on the radiance of each part; the reader must feel that every fragment as it comes provides proof of its own relevance in its illustrative power, or at least in its comic or pathetic or satiric intensity. For me only about half of the characters provide this kind of self-justification. There are many great things: moments of introspection, including some masterful dreams, from the advanced young woman and the faded beauty; moments of clear and effective observation of viciousness and folly. But too often one finds, when the tour of the passenger list is undertaken again and again, that it is too much altogether. Why, why did Miss Porter feel that she should try to get everything in? Did she really think that it would be more powerful to give forty instances of depravity than twenty, or five? . . . it is only because she tries for a canvas large and busy enough to defeat the imaginative genius of a Shakespeare that she gets into trouble.

Trouble is too strong a word. Even if all of my reservations are sound, which I doubt, the book is more worth having than most fully-successful but less ambitious novels. . . . What I hope most of all is that you'll find me completely mistaken in asking for a more rigorous or an inappropriate economy, and that, unlike those who have praised the novel in public so far, you'll explain to me how to read it better on my next try. For now, honesty requires a timid vote of admiring, almost shamefaced disappointment.[2]

Since a useful version of Aristotle's *Poetics* has been available to us, there have been critics who have been engaged in what has been called criticism proper, the task of determining what literature in general is, and what a given work of literature in particular is. One fundamental assumption of criticism proper is that by a more and more refined classification, according to a work's properties, all literature can be first divided into kinds and sub-kinds. Ideally, and as such a process becomes more and more discriminating and precise, and as the subdivisions become smaller and smaller, criticism will approach the individual work. Accordingly the proper critic assumes that all questions of evaluation, including, of course, moral evaluation, are secondary to and issue from questions of definition. Or to phrase it otherwise, the proper critic asks: "How can we tell what a work means, let alone whether it's good or bad, if we don't know what it is to begin with?" At this point, I call attention to the fact that in none of my own references to *Ship of Fools* have I spoken of it as a novel. The *Commentary* editor calls it a novel and Booth calls it a novel and in the very process of describing what it is about this alleged novel that displeases them, they go a long way toward unintentionally defining the work as something else altogether. But instead of evaluating *Ship of Fools* on the grounds of their own description of its properties, both insist on ignoring these analytical data, making two substitutions in their stead: (1) the publisher's word for it that *Ship of Fools* is a novel and (2) their own bias as to how the work would have to be written to have been acceptable as a novel. Booth is both candid and disarming in making explicit his bias for finely constructed, concentrated plots. To entertain a preference for *Pride and Prejudice* or *The Great Gatsby* over, say, *Moby Dick* or *Finnegans Wake* is one thing and legitimate enough in its way. To insist, however, that the latter two works are inferior because their integrity does not depend on traditional plot structure would be to risk downgrading two admittedly monumental works in a very arbitrary and dubious way. To insist that every long work of prose fiction should be as much like *Pride and Prejudice* as possible is to insist that

15

every such work be not only a novel but a nineteenth-century one at that.

The *Commentary* critique has its own bias, of course, which is not stated explicitly. It is the bias of the journal itself as much as of the critic, and is one it shares with many another respectable publication whose voice is directed at an audience it understands to have a highly developed, "independent," post-Freudian, post-Marxist, humanitarian social consciousness. Neither especially visionary nor especially doctrinaire, such a publication has, typically, a low tolerance for anything that smacks of the concept of original sin, having, as this concept does, a way of discouraging speculation about decisively improving the human lot. Miss Porter's book appeared to take a dim view of the behavior of the race and that is enough for the intellectual journal, despite its implied claim to having broad views and cultivated interests, including an interest in fiction. The aggrieved critic cannot come down from high dudgeon long enough to see that a view of literature as merely an ideological weapon is, in the first place, a strangely puritanical one and wildly out of place in his pages. In the second place, there are a few more commonplaces about literature which are usually lost sight of in the urgency to claim that people are not all bad and therefore can and must be portrayed in fiction as likely candidates for salvation. Most works of fiction are not written to produce anything but themselves, but some works of fiction are written to demonstrate to the innocent that there is much evil in the world. And others are written to demonstrate to the initiated, but phlegmatic, that there is more evil than even they had supposed and that this evil is closer to home than they can comfortably imagine. In any case, since fiction is by definition artificial, the author is within his rights in appearing to overstate the case for the desired results. It is nowhere everlastingly written that literature must have a sanguine, optimistic, and uplifting effect. Is there not sometimes something salutary in a work which has the effect of inducing disgust and functioning therefore as a kind of emetic? Had the critic given Miss Porter her due as an artist, he might have seen that *Ship of Fools* condemns human folly, but it never once confuses good and evil. It is one thing to be a writer who smirks at human decency and argues for human destruction (de Sade, say), it is another to be a writer who winces at human limitations and pleads by her tone, by her attitude toward her readers, for a pained nod of agreement. Said Dr. Johnson to the Honorable Thomas Erskine some two hundred years ago: "Why sir, if you were to read Richardson for the story, your impatience would be so much fretted that you would hang yourself. But you must read him for the sentiment." In the case of *Ship of Fools,* this sentiment is so consistent and so pervasive as to make us wonder how anyone could have scanted or mistaken it. It is the very opposite of misanthropy in that far from taking delight in exposing human foibles, in "getting" her characters' "number," Miss Porter's narrative voice has the quality of personal suffering even as it gives testimony. It seems to say: "This is the way with the human soul, as I knew it, at its worst, in the years just prior to the Second World War. And alas for all of us that it should have been so." By way of illustration, recall the characters Ric and Rac. I select them because Miss Porter's readers of all stripes agree that these two children, scarcely out of their swaddling clothes, are probably as thoroughly objectionable as any two fictional characters in all literature in English. Twin offspring of a pimp and a prostitute, they lie, steal, torture, attempt to murder a dumb animal, cause the death of an innocent man, and fornicate incestuously; they are not very convincing as ordinary children and for a very good reason. They are not meant to be. I cite a passage from that section where, having made a fiasco of their parents' larcenous schemes, they are punished by those parents:

Tito let go of Rac and turned his fatherly discipline upon Ric. He seized his right arm by the wrist and twisted it very slowly and steadily until the shoulder was nearly turned in its socket and Ric went to his knees with a long howl that died away in a puppy-like whimper when the terrible hold was loosed. Rac, huddled on the divan nursing her bruises, cried again with him. Then Manolo and Pepe and Tito and Pancho, and Lola and Concha and Pastora and Amparo, every face masking badly a sullen fright, went away together to go over every step of this dismaying turn of affairs; with a few words and nods, they decided it would be best to drink coffee in the bar, to appear as usual at dinner, and to hold a rehearsal on deck afterwards. They were all on edge and ready to fly at each other's throats. On her way out, Lola paused long enough to seize Rac by the hair and shake her head until she was silenced, afraid to cry. When they were gone, Ric and Rac crawled into the upper berth looking for safety; they lay there half naked, entangled like some afflicted, misbegotten little monster in a cave, exhausted, mindless, soon asleep.[3] (360)

For some 357 pages, a case has been carefully built for the twins' monstrous natures. The reader has been induced to loathe the very sound of their names. Suddenly the same reader finds himself an eyewitness to the degree of punishment he has privately imagined they deserved. But even as they are being terribly chastised, they demonstrate an admirable recalcitrance and suddenly it is the adult world that appears villainous, monstrous, and cruel. In the imagery of our last view of them, they are not demons altogether, or even primarily, but in their nakedness, which we see first, they are also merely infants and this is what does—or should—break the reader's heart. The reader is meant to sympathize, finally, with these hideous children but, more than that, his moral responses have been directed to himself. He has been led to ask himself: "Who am I that I should have for so long despised these children, however demonic they are? Am I, then, any better than their parents?"

When I contend that Ric and Rac are not meant to be taken for ordinary children, I am agreeing for the moment with the *Commentary* critic who spoke of Miss Porter's method of characterization as caricature, as if to speak of this method so were, *ipso facto*, to condemn it; as if realism were the only possible fictional mode and the only category in which a long fiction can be cast. But if *Ship of Fools* is not a novel, what would a novel be? I rely on the recent study by Sheldon Sacks, *Fiction and the Shape of Belief* (Berkeley, 1964), to define it as follows: a novel would be "an action organized so that it introduces characters about whose fates the reader is made to care, in unstable relationships, which are then further complicated, until the complication is finally resolved, by the removal of the represented instability." This plainly is not *Ship of Fools.* Our most human feelings go out to Ric and Rac, but we cannot care further about them, *not* because we are made to hate them but because they are clearly doomed to perpetual dehumanization by the adult world that spawned and nurtured them. In the same image in which Miss Porter represents them as helpless infants, she also declares them "mindless." The generally unstable relationships which define the roles of most of the other characters in the book remain unstable to the very end and are not so much resolved as they are revealed. The resolution of the manifold conflicts in the work is part of the encompassing action of the work, that which the reader can logically suppose will happen after the story closes. The Germans will march against Poland and turn Europe into an inferno. The others will, until it is too late, look the other way. This is a fact of history which overrides in importance the fact that no one on the ship can possibly come to good.

Nor is *Ship of Fools* a satire as Sacks defines it, that is, organized so that it ridicules objects external to the fictional world created in it. Rather it is, I believe, in Sacks's terms, a kind of modern apologue, a work organized as a fictional example of the truth of a formulable statement or a series of such statements.[4] As such it owes more than its title to the didactic Christian verses of Sebastian Brant, whose *Das Narrenschiff* [The ship of fools] was published sometime between 1497 and 1548. Brant's work was very influential and no one thinks of it as misanthropic when he reads:

> The whole world lives in darksome night,
> In blinded sinfulness persisting,
> While every street sees fools existing
> Who know but folly, to their shame,
> Yet will not own to folly's name.
> Hence I have pondered how a ship
> Of fools I'd suitably equip—
> A galley, brig, bark, skiff, or float,
> A carack, scow, dredge, racing-boat,
> A sled, cart, barrow, caryall—
> One vessel would be far too small
> to carry all the fools I know.
> Some persons have no way to go
> And like the bees they come a-skimming,
> While many to the ship are swimming,
> Each one wants to be the first,
> A mighty throng with folly curst,
> Whose pictures I have given here.
> They who at writings like to sneer
> Or are with reading not afflicted
> May see themselves herewith depicted
> And thus discover who they are,
> Their faults, to whom they're similar.
> For fools a mirror shall it be,
> Where each his counterfeit may see.[5]

As an apologue Miss Porter's work has more in common with Johnson's *Rasselas* than with *Gone with the Wind*. As an apologue it not only has the right, it has the function by its nature to "caricature" its actors, to be "saturnine," to have a large cast, to be "fragmented" in its narration, and above all, to quote Booth again, to achieve "unity based on theme and idea rather than coherence of action . . . [to have] no steady center of interest except the progressively more intense exemplification of its central truth. . . ."

In addition to calling attention to its formal properties for evaluating Miss Porter's book not as a novel but as something else, one ought to stand back a bit to see how the work fits a reasonable definition of the novel historically, that is, according to traditional and conventional themes and types of action. Recall that though the English word *novel*, to designate a kind of fiction, is derived from the Italian *novella*, meaning "a little new thing," this is not the word used in most European countries. That word is, significantly, *roman*. One forgets that a work of fiction, set in our own time and thus bringing us knowledge of our own time, that is, news, is not a novel by that fact alone, but may be a literary form as yet undefined and, therefore, unnamed. For, in addition to bringing us news, the novel, if it is such on historical principles, must pay its respects to its forebears in more than a nominal way. It must do more than bear tales and look like the *Brothers Karamazov*. It must, I suspect, as a *roman*, be in some specific ways romantic.

We understand that the novel is the modern counterpart of various earlier forms of extended narrative. The earliest of these, the epic, was succeeded in the Middle Ages by the *romance* first written, like the epic, in verse and later in prose. The romance told of the adventures of royalty and the nobility, introduced a heroine, and made love a central theme. It relocated the supernatural realm from the court of Zeus to fairyland. The gods were replaced by magical spells and enchantments. When magical spells and enchantments were replaced, in the precursors of contemporary fiction, by the happy accident, the writer took unto himself a traditional given and the romantic tradition continued in the novel. When Henry James arranged for his heroine Isabel Archer to inherit a substantial sum of money from a relative who did not know her, it was very Olympian of him; at any rate

21

it was a piece of modern magic, legitimately granted to the novelist. Realist though he was, James recognized that the romantic element gets the novel going, frees the hero or heroine from those confinements of everyday life which make moral adventure undramatic. When in the most arbitrary way James makes Isabel an heiress, he launches her on a quest for self-realization. He gives her her chance. Now in this connection, I quote again from *Ship of Fools:*

> While [Freytag] shaved he riffled through his ties and selected one, thinking that people on voyage mostly went on behaving as if they were on dry land, and there is simply not room for it on a ship. Every smallest act shows up more clearly and looks worse, because it has lost its background. The train of events leading up to and explaining it is not there; you can't refer it back and set it in its proper size and place. (132)

When Miss Porter, who could have put her cast of characters anywhere she wanted, elected to put them aboard ship, she made as if to free them, in the manner of a romance, for a moral quest; that is, they are ostensibly liberated, as if by magic, precisely because they *are* aboard ship—liberated from the conventions of family background, domestic responsibility, national custom, and race consciousness. Theoretically, they can emerge triumphant over duplicity, cruelty, selfishness, and bigotry at the end of the journey. But they do not.

Freedom they are incapable of utilizing for humane ends. Freedom Miss Porter can grant them, but since they are men of our time, they cannot, in her view, accept it responsibly. That is, they cannot make good use of their lucky accident because their freedom is only nominal. On the one hand, history has caught up with them; on the other hand, psychology has stripped their spiritual and emotional lives of all mystery. In Miss Porter's world the past is merely the genesis of neurosis (there is no point in pretending we have never heard of Freud) and the future, quite simply, is the destruction of Isabel Archer's Europe of infinite possibilities (there is no point in pretending we have never heard of Neville Chamberlain). *Ship of Fools* argues that romantic literary conventions do not work in the modern world, and emerges as even more remote from the idea of the novel than a study of its formal properties alone would suggest. One can see it finally as anti-novel.

In her 1940 introduction to "Flowering Judas," Miss Porter says that she spent most of her "energies" and "spirit" in an effort to understand "the logic of this majestic and terrible failure of man in the Western world." This is the dominant theme of *Ship of Fools* as it is of nearly all her writing. Nearly every character in the work is a staggering example of an aspect of this failure. And here is the only thematic passage in the work emphasized by italics:

> *What they were saying to each other was only, love me, love me in spite of all! Whether or not I love you, whether I am fit to love, whether you are able to love, even if there is no such thing as love, love me.* (480)

II

When her most faithful readers were disappointed in Miss Porter's *Ship of Fools,* feeling that, after all, they had waited in vain for something in the work to happen, they failed to see that it had been happening all the while, as it does typically in the modern short story, at least since Joyce. This is quite to the point because these readers conceded that Miss Porter had emerged, as many commentators had averred, an unreconstructed short-story writer whose efforts to compose a much longer work yielded at best a "classic *manqué*," and at worst a dull, misanthropic, commonplace novel. In any case, what she had written was seen as notably lacking in the magic of the early short pieces on which her reputation was made and on which her fame, it now seemed, would have to rest.

One reason that *Ship of Fools* has been criticized in many ways as a bad *novel,* likened to a single badly attenuated short story, or beheld as a tedious and directionless aggregate of many short stories in a single setting with a common cast of characters, is the failure to see that the employment by its author of modern short-story strategies was not only appropriate but indispensable to the realized intention of *Ship of Fools,* insofar as its stories correspond to the incidents and episodes of the traditional apologue. Moreover, the work has more direction than meets the biased eye.

I had already affirmed the commonplace that it is singularly poor criticism to evaluate a work adversely on the basis of formal properties seen to be lacking, while at once ignoring those properties that are present, especially when they are present in a discernible order and to an effective end, when I discovered Paul W. Miller's rather typical strictures.[6] I find them useful points of departure for some observations on character and method in *Ship of Fools,* and I hope their substance will further clear away some of the confusion about what Miss Porter has, in fact, done, and about the propriety of what she has done for a special kind of lengthy fiction.

Miller's argument-from-genre is that a novel, by virtue of its magnitude, requires a kind of attention to characterization not required of the short story. Of characterization in *Ship of Fools* he contends for two putative defects: undifferentiated characters, that is, characters who so closely resemble each other "as to invite confusion"; and indecorous characters, that is, characters who are "overdeveloped in view of the slight part they play . . . in the two principal events of the novel—the ostracism of Freytag and the temporary coup of the *zarzuela* dancers." He concludes: "These defects of characterization point to significant weaknesses in Miss Porter's novel. The first of these is a weakness in construction. It is a failure on the part of a great short story writer to adapt her materials perfectly to the very different requirements of the novel." The second alleged significant weakness, if I construe Miller correctly, is of Miss Porter's craftsmanship, rooted in her presumed naturalistic stance. It is this which leads Miss Porter, according to Miller, to characterize Captain Thiele poorly, in that he comports himself not according to the demands of the "novel" but according to Miss Porter's view of "society as being made up of clusters of individuals illustrating certain basic types." He does, therefore, "inconsistently" yield to the criminal pressures of the zarzuela company, in contradiction of his character as an early *donné* in the work.

I will first address myself to certain errors in Miller's argument which I think are attributable to his presuppositions (the basic one being that *Ship of Fools* is a novel) and then to his ensuing expectations, perforce unsatisfied. There are perhaps fifty, but at least four (not two) principal events in the book. In addition to the Freytag and zarzuela stories, there is that of Etchegaray, the Basque woodcarver, who (to the monumental indifference of the non-steerage principals) gives his life to rescue a dog owned by two of the many contemptible characters. The beating of Denny by Mrs. Treadwell as part of the all-important *walpurgisnacht* episodes is a fourth. It is significant, however, that virtually any particular grouping of episodes could itself as well be read as constituting a principal event, depending on how arbitrarily one elects to read one segment of narrative as discrete from another in a work which is characterized by its singleness of intention, and more by its measured linear progression toward debarkation, than by dramatic peaks on the voyage itself. This is crucial, inasmuch as Miller has spoken of the "movement" of the work, to which he has found the characterization inadequate. Etchegaray would be, on Miller's scale, an "underdeveloped" character, seen as he is not from the inside but only from above-decks. However, in what has passed for a "novel of character," but is in fact a fiction in which character is the method of presentation of varieties of foolishness (quite a different thing), it makes little difference whether characters are "overdeveloped" or "underdeveloped," whether they duplicate each other, whether they behave consistently or otherwise, or whether they contribute to the forward motion of the action in proportion to their degree of characterization, because their function in the work is less to act out a plot than to represent a set of ideas, in this case venial sins calamitous in their effect.

Neither the sins nor the characters' embodiment of those sins are in need of proof, for both are the givens of the work. Herr Reiber, for example, despite Miss Porter's exposing his character in a straightforward manner, is on the scene not primarily to contribute to effecting an outcome, as is, say, Tom Buchanan in *The Great Gatsby,* but to behave swinishly in respect to other humans, *at any and every given moment,* so as to represent swinishness itself. It is simply that however much Miss Porter might be committed, in theory, to that variety of naturalism associated with Stephen Crane, as Miller asserts, she has not, in any case in *Ship of Fools,* elected to let her story "tell itself" in the manner of Zola. Her methods are markedly aesthetic, befitting a writer who subscribes also to the conscious craftmanship (the dominance of the writer over the material) of Henry James. Herr Reiber is natural enough, but that variety of nature that most distinguishes him is to be seen reflected in the face not of a man but of a pig. It is as such that he is made to be seen by the reader. His inamorata is a peahen. The point is that the author of a naturalistic novel *presents* the swinishness of people as typically human; the author of a realistic apologue *represents* the conduct of humans as typically swinish.

The immutable aspect of Miss Porter's beast epic characters, given at the outset, defines their proper relationship to the movement of the work. This movement, which certainly does not depend on a Sophoclean structure, will not satisfy every neoclassical insistence on a beginning, a middle, and an end. Nevertheless, the action of *Ship of Fools* builds, classically enough, to the zarzuela party episodes where the passengers, now literally masked, are seen to undergo a significant unmasking, but it falls off to a kind of denouement which is not, strictly speaking, an unraveling. No unraveling of complex relationships is called for in *Ship of Fools* any more than it is called for in the stories from *Dubliners* and for the same reason. In both instances, what has come to be understood as the hallmark of the modern short story, a resolution cradled subtly in the course of the story's slow-rising and muted "action," is the work's larger pattern.

Because *Ship of Fools* combines a series of stories and, overall, employs the shape of the short story, it is to that degree *like* a short story in that it strives for a single effect. But because it only resembles a short story and is in fact something else, it strives for that effect many times in many combinations of characters and in greater degrees of dramatic intensity until its conclusion. The single effect, apprehended by the reader as a presentiment of impending war and moral disaster, is the theme of helpless folly, the prime characteristic of the most quotidian human contacts. This is announced without bashfulness in the didactic and fabulous title.

Miss Porter's method is to dramatize the theme in a microcosmic setting (the ship) with a cast of contemporary types, on a traditional, mythic quest (the journey home). The mode of dramatization is the symbolic narrative

27

realism of the modern short story, whereby the writer depicts a world of recognizable norms of behavior, in a verifiable setting, but with such a scrupulous selectivity that the most commonplace actions and objects take on an allegorical function. The design of the work is the arrangement of a number of stories, some of greater magnitude than others, most of them touching upon the others, but all of them related if only slightly, if only by tone and feeling, to the end that the reader is overcome by the work's insistence. *Ship of Fools* insists on the single fact that sentimentality, weakness, cruelty, and irresponsibility have flourished too long in the name of love. (The zarzuela coup is not at all "temporary.") This insistence is achieved in great measure not only by a necessary proliferation of characters and character types but by a special juxtaposition of stories, which gives the work an appropriately ironic texture. It is achieved also by a characteristic expositional logic within the stories juxtaposed, and, finally, by an attention to language in excess of the exclusively narrative demands of an ordinary extended fiction.

The scene, for example, in which Jenny proposes in vain to her sulky lover David that they invite Freytag to take his meals at their table,[7] is notably typical in that it appears to figure structurally, in its time and place of appearance, as merely a way of giving the reader yet another brief dreary chapter in the feckless relationship of the pair and to provide, in addition, a removed view of Freytag soon after his unconscionable banishment by the proto-Nazis. He is seen by Jenny at the other side of the bar in the company of Mrs. Treadwell, "the two of them quite untroubled and good-looking." But in other ways it is significantly much more. Initially, it is a short story in itself, capable of standing alone outside the book. As a story, its function is to define the relationship between two people. In the context of *Ship of Fools,* however, where Freytag is more than simply

28

banished—he is banished for motives which prefigure the historic fact of genocide—it cradles the entire work's "outcome," that enveloping action which is not part of the action itself but the action to which the entire work persistently points. For when Jenny rationalizes her sexual jealousy at the sight of Freytag and an attractive woman by saying, "Every day I learn something about something else that is none of my business," [8] she is, of course, understood to be precisely wrong, as history first and then Miss Porter's book, in its own way, have proved. But it is remarkable that the weighty function of this "short story"—and it has this much in common with virtually all the stories in the book—is not in the foreground. What is in the foreground is, deceptively, only the required inquiry into a "love" affair that is based altogether on self-love and self-hatred.

What the story signifies beyond what it depicts, however, is in the realm of ethical belief on a world scale. This belief, that avoidance of collective responsibility invites collective disaster, subsumes one story after another and imparts to the work its thematic unity. The connection between such emotional poverty and the universally destructive behavior which issues from it is realized at the conclusion of the book: the *Vera* lands in Germany and not somewhere else. This same connection, moreover, inheres in nearly every story, rounded out as the work is, because Bremerhaven, as the port of debarkation, is immediately given, and because the *Vera* is a ship and not a wayward bus. Short of sinking, it will get there, and no one can get out and walk. The connection, then, between Miss Porter's stories and the outcome of the work is as firmly constructed as anyone has the right to expect. This follows if the reader observes that the meaningfulness of *Ship of Fools* is played out again and again, and that the arrival at Bremerhaven is not, as it might be in a novel, a turn of events; that it is, rather, the figurative setting for the last reiteration of theme.

Jenny's proposal to extend to Freytag a gesture of humane generosity is, first of all, insincerely prompted. Freytag is, Miss Porter intrudes to say, "a pretext" for a quarrel. In their unwholesome relationship only quarreling and making up can keep Jenny and David together, for there is no other basis for their liaison. Moreover, making David jealous is part of this tawdry game. And being jealous, on David's part, is equally a gambit. Finally, a bit of cheating, on Jenny's part, is not only a way of making David jealous but is an all-important means to a necessary self-abasement. When Jenny sees her all-purpose foil, Freytag, apparently in no need of her inasmuch as he has the attention of the attractive Mrs. Treadwell, gone are both Freytag's usefulness and the need for generous gestures. It is a simple matter now for her to contrive yet another mask for herself. This time she will disguise herself as the non-meddler. Thus we see the way in which the dubious virtue of minding one's own business (when others need to have their business minded) merges with the work's total thematic effect.

To summarize: a self-contained short story has here functioned in four distinct but interrelated ways: (1) to advance the work's surface action (what is happening now to Freytag, Mrs. Treadwell, David, and Jenny?); (2) to dramatize the psychological truth of the relationship among four characters; (3) to serve, perhaps in Coleridge's sense of the organic, as bud to the tree, insofar as the truth of their motives will, in the end, bring down upon the "lovers" the moral judgment of history; and (4) to foreshadow the literal masking and figurative unmasking of the zarzuela fiesta, itself a correlative for the work's entire masking and unmasking, concealment and exposure.[9] This kind of working connection, no less than the ship's progress, is the movement of the book, culminating in those scenes in which, ironically, fools wearing the disguises of sensible men and women put on the costumes of other fools, thinking they are at a masquerade.

The kind of logical, causal-temporal relationships one has a right to expect from what has traditionally been designated the novel is present in the foreground of the work, but only little more than, say, in *Candide,* where likewise one has no right to insist on its prominence. This is the case inasmuch as Candide's adventures, like those of the characters in *Ship of Fools,* are fabricated to reiterate a fool's deportment and to imply its meaning, not to dramatize fully the myriad probabilities, possibilities, and likelihoods of human action.

Finally, however, those commentators who hastened to see in Miss Porter's strategies the failure of the novelist might have put aside their presuppositions long enough to see what the stories did, because short stories, they were very willing to allow, do things only in their own way. They might have recalled, for instance, that the short story writer often depends on language to do the job of the novelist's plot. When Miss Porter describes Freytag and Mrs. Treadwell as, from Jenny's view, "quite untroubled and good-looking," she is outreaching the novelist's narrative description. She is showing Freytag's mask, the mask of a man not really untroubled, but in the worst trouble the world has ever known.

III

In the introduction to *Ship of Fools,* Miss Porter recalls that she read Sebastian Brant's *Das Narrenschiff* in 1932, with her European voyage (Veracruz to Bremerhaven, 1931) recently behind her. Aboard ship she had kept a diary, the source of more extensive notes to be made the next year. The actual composition of the fiction in the form of a working draft began in 1941 at Yaddo.[10] Until now inaccessible, a letter from Miss Porter to Malcolm Cowley in 1931 seems genetic in its position between the diary and conscious labor on the work. It tends, moreover, to support a reading of *Ship of Fools* as an apologue [11] by felicitous predisposition rather than as a novel by misguided intention. It has been in great measure by the latter reading that the critical reception of *Ship of Fools* has been generally unfavorable. The entire letter follows:

> Berlin, September 25, 1931
> Care American Consulate-General, Bellevuestrasse 8,
> Dear Malcolm:
>
> For the moment, I am settled permanently in a stuffy little hotel, the Thuringer Hof, on Hedemanstrasse, near enough to all sorts of things, but not noisy, for a city. . . . The tale of how I landed here when I was firmly on my way to the south of Italy through Paris is simple enough: Only a North German Lloyd tramp steamer was leaving Vera Cruz at the very time I had to leave, or go through a long rigamarole of having my Mexican permit extended. So we got German visas, and decided on Berlin. Our boat rambled all over the world for twenty-seven days, past Cuba, the Caribbean Islands, Teneriffe, the coast of Africa, two ports in Spain, and even stopped at Boulogne, when the captain was swearing all the way he would not stop there, on to Southampton, and so up the muddy Weser to Bremen; we tore our hair at all the ports where we could have left that boat if the agent had not deceived us, leading us into having only a German visa to start out with.[12]
>
> I had wanted to come to Berlin, but not just yet. We are here, and I am well finished with travel for the time being. Living is very cheap here, this hotel has steam heat, and I am collecting odds and ends of wool garments against the cold. It is enlivening to be in a city once more, and easier to stay indoors and work a little. I wrote the first draft of a short story on the boat, and in these two days have finished it up and have begun a poem. The manuscript of the novel is still packed away, but it will come out in a few days. . . .
>
> The second day, I went to a bookshop and ordered Mrs. Woolf's

novel,[13] so it will be here by Monday at least. I will send on that review quickly. The Paris mail has been sent for, and I am watching for the New Republic for my Chase review. . . .[14] There was more I could have said, maybe more explicitly, but it seemed useless. It is no good wasting critical energy on worthless books. The best of it was published in the N. R. and his whole idea was worth that series of articles and no more.

Here I feel the atmosphere of great poverty, strain, and thrift, with prices for food counted in odd pfennings, great numbers of men in early middle age with scarred, mended heads, glass eyes, artificial legs and arms; but few beggars; [15] and the street women who come out after ten o'clock at night are very fresh-faced and young and well-dressed. . . . I have not seen anything but the center of town, from Unter den Linden down to Belle-Alliance Platz and round about. I am badly dressed but so is everyone. I am not expected to be rich, and that is very comfortable for me, because I am tired of never having enough to live on. There is night life, and cabarets, and a few French shops, but I need not feel I am missing the tone of the place if I never go near them. . . . Last night in a little restaurant we were eating our tremendous plates of red cabbage and meat and potatoes, when a whining sour voice drolled out of the radio:

"It makes me feeeel so bloo
When you saaaaay adew!"

The waiter explained that it was a famous American jazz orchestra broadcasting from a cabaret nearby, and gave us the address, certain that we were going there at once.

When I grow afraid of the cold, I take comfort that four million persons are living here through the winter, and so will I. Now I want only to get some work done, and here is as good a place as any, and now is the time.

Did you see Eugene Jolas? I wish to see him once again at least, to tell him the story of what happened when I went to see Gottfried Benn, carrying Eugene's letter and I will tell you sometime when I am not so hurried. . . . Well, he speaks only French and German, and I speak only Spanish and English, so that is enough of a plot. . . . It was only that I went in serious hopes of saying something I wished to say, and of hearing him say certain things I had been told he would say in a particularly interesting manner. . . . We were happy to see each other in four languages, not one of which matched, then we drank coffee and made

33

helpless gestures at each other, and were both pretty exhausted at the end of half an hour. . . . When he spoke French I could understand, but could not answer, and that was even worse. . . .

1st moral: Never present letters of introduction
2nd moral: Never go to Europe without a working knowledge
of French.

Do you have any friends here? Tell me their names, but no letters. Only if I should happen to run across them. That is much better.

I had a letter from Peggy [16] full of woes such as can happen in Mexico: the one that made the most lasting impression on us both was that she sat on a freshly painted toilet, got a green ring on her little behind, and as the bathroom heater is out of repair, she must wait for time to repair this disaster. . . .

The surface of this place is all a welter of feather beds, over-stuffed furniture, men and women shaped like something by Albrecht Dürer, great masses of sculpture full of senseless energy without direction, hanging dangerously off every cornice and facade—streets like burnished iron and great platters of cheap harsh food. But later I may be able to tell you about the new houses, and the new music and painting, even the literature . . . one will be a clew to the other.

Give me news of yourself, remember me to anyone who asks of me. I hope now really to be able to send you some small sketches of the kind you asked for. There are many waiting to be done.

Love,
Katherine Anne [17]

In *Ship of Fools*, Veracruz is "a little purgatory between land and sea," [18] and it is the burden of the work to dramatize the fact that, given their natures, the *Vera's* passengers will not improve their lot by sailing to Bremerhaven, since they carry with them the painful and grotesque underworld of their lives. Germany holds for them only calamity, because Miss Porter's Germans, fancying their homeland to be "promised," carry with them from Mexico fantasies of violence.

That the voyage, as described to Mr. Cowley, was,

in fact, a limbo, where Miss Porter and her associates could want to "tear their hair" in frustration, not only provided the feeling for the fictional reconstruction but presented her with an actual experience ready-made for allegorical use. She could adapt it whole to depict an existence at once very much of this world and at a remove from it, for life aboard any ship is, perforce, artificial.

The reader is induced to see the characters of *Ship of Fools* as both particularly and generally natural. The story becomes didactic, cautionary, as one sees himself among the fools. An *allegoria* builds in the sense of the work's appearing to bear a meaning, only to insist on further interpretation. Taken together, Miss Porter's revealing that she had not wanted to go to Germany at the time, and her contemptuous allusion to the commercial jazz band as a token of American vulgarity, define her in 1931 as, by temperament, an exile, quite as rootless as her fictional characters. The difference, however, is aesthetic. She sees herself as she is, a citizen of the community of letters only. The *Vera's* passengers, on the other hand, have no such refuge, but are unaware. A certain wisdom permitted her to see the ship as metaphor. In another unpublished letter, expressing annoyance at persons who want to know where she *is* in her writing, Miss Porter reminds her correspondent that she writes fiction and is, therefore, everywhere.[19]

Commentators have, in the main, curiously refused to take Miss Porter's word that she owes something to the inspiration of Brant's verses. When they have, they have usually taken it too literally. It seems indicated from the date of her letter to Mr. Cowley that Miss Porter's view of the human spectacle had been remarkably similar, morally and aesthetically, to Brant's all along; that her reading of *Das Narrenschiff*, after her trip to Germany, had merely discovered for her a kindred literary spirit. She proceeded then to employ with a surface realism the same traditional image of the ship of life. One is also led to this conclusion, especially, by her reference to Dürer.

Since probably she had not as yet seen *Das Narrenschiff*, Miss Porter presumably did not know that Dürer had illustrated it. Yet she could observe of Germany that "the surface of this place is all a welter of feather beds, overstuffed furniture, men and women shaped like something by Albrecht Dürer. . . ." Most telling in this is Miss Porter's strikingly literary way of seeing the Germans. She sees them as representations rather than presentations. They are less persons than fictionalized figures and types. As in the fiction she was later to write, she notes their grossness as it stands for and embodies her conception of them. It is less surprising, in light of this, that Miss Porter was inclined to write a modern version of the beast epic.

Chapter 2
The Composition of "Old Mortality"

I

"Do you remember the little set of three short novels,[1] *Noon Wine, Old Mortality,* and *Pale Horse, Pale Rider?*" Miss Porter asked an interviewer in 1964,[2] as if they could have slipped his mind, those three crystalline tales, so hard and clear, yet sometimes so perplexing. "When I signed a contract for these stories I had had them in mind for years. Then all of a sudden, it's like an egg forming, they were ready to go. So I went to see my publisher and said I'm ready now to make[3] those stories that we were talking about. They gave me a contract for four[4] short novels and so I took my little notes and papers and went up to the country and sat down in a little inn and wrote the first one in seven days[5]—'Old Mortality.'"

The gestation period for most writers is notoriously lengthy; this, together with Miss Porter's disarming admission that she was not one of those who could "flourish" in the twenties and thirties, "a period of grotesque dislocations in a whole society when the world was heaving in the sickness of a millennial change,"[6] can account for a relatively modest output; one, nevertheless, which gained for her a lofty critical reputation if not a broad popular one, and generally without benefit of much proper literary examination. Norman Mailer could now say with irony unintended, "Well, you know, there was a time when I wanted very much to belong to the literary world. I wanted to be respected the way someone like Katherine Anne Porter used to be respected."[7]

An author's pronouncements on his own work we know to be often unreliable, and this unreliability extends as well to the details of his career. "Old Mortality" is such a "made" work, so sure in its language, so realized in its apparent aims, that one is tempted to be skeptical of its author's claim to have finished it off in a week. An examination of the first draft, however, leads one to take Miss Porter's word for it; so does a comparison of the first draft with the authorized published version.[8] Finally, such an examination is of some help in getting at the work's meaning about which there is disagreement enough.

On the title page of the first draft, below the title itself, is a three-paragraph introductory note in Miss Porter's hand, dated June 7, 1939. I assume it was written on the occasion of her making a gift of the document to the University of Texas. It tells us that what is to follow is a first draft made from notes which were destroyed, and that from this first draft, subsequently "corrected," the final copy was made. It says that the final draft and galley proofs are the property of the *Southern Review* in which "Old Mortality" was published in Spring, 1937.[9] She concludes with the information, not entirely accessible in the work itself, that the story is set in "that section between Austin and San Marcos, known as Hays County, and in New Orleans."

This sixty-five leaf typescript is remarkably uncluttered because there are no major structural revisions and few of the less strategic variety, but some of the latter are rather helpful. The closest to a genuine alteration in the story proper is at the point where Miranda is giving cousin Eva her version of the episode in which her father, Harry, has taken a shot at the young Creole who, it seemed, compromised Cousin Amy. In handwritten interlineations (leaf 53), Miss Porter changed the focus from Gabriel to Miranda's father; the revision establishes Miranda's belief that her father acted on his own to save Gabriel from a duel. In the original version, Gabriel is supposed to have feared that if he shot the young man, Amy would refuse to marry him because of it, and the notion was abroad (a lie in Miranda's view) that Gabriel had put Harry up to it.

When Maria and Miranda meet Uncle Gabriel for the first time, he is a "vast bulging man with a red face," not at all the romantic figure who would have died for love of Amy; who indeed once wrote "tombstone" verse [10] on the occasion of her death; who was once a dashing, reckless cavalier, about whom the family never ceased to talk as if he were still a handsome twenty-one. The girls are shocked nearly out of their wits at the discrepancy between fact and legend. They could scarcely breathe. In the first draft (leaf 32), "they grew quite breathless with disappointment." Miss Porter, it turns out, was not satisfied with this. Nor presumably would Flaubert have been, but in a different way. He would somehow have rendered their breathlessness, as he did Emma Bovary's dizziness, by planting early in the work something like Binet's lathe to make the breathlessness objective. The reader would recognize the familiar, and the breathlessness would be felt. Miss Porter, however, is not always that kind of a "modern" and in this instance she had something else in mind. "They were quite breathless with disappointment" is typed over and in its place she has written in ink, "Oh, what did grown-up people *mean* when they talked, anyway?" For the overwhelming quality of the girls' emotions there is thus substituted the sensible quality of the reader's mind, a reader who Miss Porter faithfully believes can have his own breath taken away by the accuracy and simplicity of a rhetoric so overt, yet so telling.

The balance of the revisions are also brief: deletions, substitutions, or insertions, three or four to a page, indicating second thoughts about the aptness or decorum of a word or phrase as determined by the work's self-consistency. For six or seven pages at a stretch one finds only typographical corrections. One can assume, I suppose, that some revisions were made on the author's proofs, even though the introductory note suggests otherwise. I am certainly aware of only one (leaf 18) of which the unrevised first draft reads:

> "I was sitting up as I always did until my children came in," the grandmother said, years later. "I saw at once that something was very wrong." "What happened Amy?" "Oh, Harry goes around shooting at people at a party," she said, sitting down as if she were exhausted.

"Years later" is deleted and "remembering" is substituted. The revision is in Miss Porter's hand. In the published version, the entire sentence in which the revision is made fails to appear. The effect of the final revision, in this instance, is to sharpen the narrative focus, which in "Old Mortality" is rather complex but has the virtue of appearing effortless. There is, at least, a narrator's consciousness, a protagonist's consciousness, and, within the voices giving expression to these minds, there are the voices, as in this example, of lesser but important characters. By dropping the sentence Miss Porter took care to rein us in a bit, so as not to let us stray too far from her central character. She did not want the grandmother, a very formidable personality, to run off with Miranda's story.

"Her method of composition," according to Robert Penn Warren, "does not, in itself, bend readily to the compromise. In many instances, a story . . . has not been composed straight off. Instead a section here and a section there has been written—little germinal scenes explored and developed." [11] As applied to "Old Mortality," Mr. Warren's observations would have to refer to Miss Porter's "little notes and papers," for the composition itself seems the next thing to "straight off." To reconstruct: from the youthful memory came the "little notes and papers," the small fruit of conscious recollection and the unconscious store of image and echo. Then, as Miss Porter said, they were "all of a sudden . . . ready." In a week's time she typed the first draft and revised it by hand for the final copy. I suppose in the course of that week she often went back to see what she had done, typing deletions and, above them, substitutions and other insertions, but never altering the original conception, never making major rearrangements. When in this way the draft was typed out, she went through it with pen, again making the same variety of minor changes. The job of composition was finished with at least one and at most a few more minor changes on author's proofsheets.

I can share in a certain limited but important sense with the editors of many journals who have perennially treated Miss Porter's work in their pages with a kind of fulsome paternal neighborliness the notion that her Southern background can be held largely accountable for what is most peculiar in her writing. She probably owes as much to having read widely in the Greeks, in all of English literature, including Joyce, James, and Yeats, and other moderns. The death of Joyce, she said, "distressed me more than any other since the death of Yeats." [12] I suspect, nevertheless, that her sureness in the act of composition has something to do with how and where she was raised.

Allan Tate asks,

How could the most backward state in the Union produce not only William Faulkner but Stark Young, Roark Bradford, and Eudora Welty—all very different from one another but all *very* Mississippi? Yeats gave the best answer to this question when he was asked how Ireland could have had a literary renascence in the first decade of this century. He said, in effect, that poverty and ignorance had made it possible. There is no real paradox in giving Yeats' answer to the same question about Mississippi after 1919. Poverty, and the ignorance that attends poverty, had isolated the common people—the Snopeses, the Varners, the Bundrens—with the result that their language retained an *illiterate* purity, uncorrupted by the "correct" English of the half-educated school-teachers, or by sociological jargon, or by the conditioned reflex language of advertising; while at the same time a small minority in Mississippi (and in other Southern states) maintained at a high level of sophistication a *literate* purity of diction based upon the old traditions of classical humanism. The majority could not read at all; a small minority could not only read but could read Latin and cap verses from Horace and Vergil. This was scarcely a democratic situation, but I daresay one must take one's literature where one finds it, under whatever social conditions will allow it to flourish.[13]

There is in this critic's rationale something of the romantic revision of Southern history for which he has been often enough rebuked; it may not be as Tate describes it, but more as Tennessee Williams sees it: the Southern writer soon comes to be such by going out of his stultified mind into a kind of narrative dream world. Still, Tate seems more correct than not. There are many things a writer can get including, especially, knowledge and, perhaps, even language; but language—one's own language—was something Miss Porter, by the time she decided to write, had. It was given to her by her family. That they were Southern probably had something to do with it. "I grew up," she has said, "in a sort of melange."

I was reading Shakespeare's sonnets when I was thirteen years old, and I'm perfectly certain that they made the most profound impression upon me of anything I ever read. For a time I knew the whole sequence by heart; now I can only remember two or three of them. That was the turning point of my life, when I read the Shakespeare sonnets, and then, all at one blow, all of Dante—in that great big book illustrated by Gustave Doré. The plays I saw on the stage, but I don't remember reading them with any interest at all. Oh, and I read all kinds of poetry—Homer, Ronsard, all the old French poets in translation. We also had a very good library of well, you might say secular philosophers. I was incredibly influenced by Montaigne when I was very young. And one day when I was about fourteen, my father led me up to a great big line of books and said, "Why don't you read this? It'll knock some of the nonsense out of you!" It happened to be the entire set of Voltaire's philosophical dictionary with notes by Smollett. And I plowed through it—it took me about five years.

And of course we read all the 18th century novelists, though Jane Austen, like Turgenev, didn't really engage me until I was quite mature. I read them both when I was very young, but I was grown up before I really took them in. And I discovered for myself *Wuthering Heights*—I think I read that book every year of my life for fifteen years. I simply adored it. Henry James and Thomas Hardy were really my introduction to modern literature: Grandmother didn't much approve of it—she thought Dickens might do, but she was a little against Mr. Thackeray; she thought he was too trivial. So that was as far as I got into the modern world until I left home.[14]

When asked, "Don't you think this background—the comparative isolation of Southern rural life, and the atmosphere of literary interest—helped to shape you as a writer?" Miss Porter, having little of this, replied,

I think it's something in the blood. We've always had great letter writers, readers, great story-tellers in our family. I've listened all my life to articulate people. They were all great story-tellers, and every story had shape and meaning and point.

But most American writers who have told us they came from a family of "great story-tellers" and had "listened all [their lives] to articulate people," seem to have been born in the last days of the last century, in a milieu at least aspiring to aristocracy, and almost invariably in the South.

In this connection it might do to look at the opening of part 2 of "Old Mortality," first in the published version and then in the first draft. The published version reads:

During vacation on their grandmother's farm, Maria and Miranda, who read as naturally and constantly as ponies crop grass, and with much the same kind of pleasure, had by some happy chance laid hold of some forbidden reading matter, brought in and left there with missionary intent, no doubt, by some Protestant cousin. (193)

One is struck by several features of the sentence, all of which can be classified under the heading of rhetoric. The sentence is, to begin with, lexically and syntactically very clear, despite its complexity. In its complexity it is fluent and periodic. To the end of periodicity, "forbidden reading matter" is brought in nearly at the conclusion, only ahead of "missionary intent" and "Protestant cousin." Sentence periodicity is a palpable representation in language of a world properly and permanently ordered. It is the world of Miranda's childhood, the world of Gabriel, Harry, Amy, and Cousin Eva. It is the world which here Miss Porter gently mocks as she prepares the reader for Miranda's less than gentle rejection of it to come. On the linguistic level, the sentence partakes exclusively of rather formal and generally polite diction, except in the instance of the sentence's only figure, a simile in which the girls' reading is likened to ponies eating grass, where the linguistic level drops to the local and the provincial. ". . . Maria and Miranda . . . read as naturally . . . as ponies crop grass" is like "ahm hongry enough to eat the ears offen a daid mule," recognizably Southern, while the rest of the sentence, subject matter aside, could have come from one of a number of nineteenth-century English novels whose authors had been raised on classical literary models and so respected the laws of unity, coherence, and emphasis. The last is the rhetorical effect of repeating *some* three times, a word sufficiently vague to endow the subject, putative sin, with the offhandedness required to establish about it an ironic tone. This tone pervades the entire paragraph and is appropriate to the crucially ambiguous way a Catholic upbringing will figure at the end of the novella.

The entire paragraph as published reads thus:

> During vacation on their grandmother's farm, Maria and Miranda, who read as naturally and constantly as ponies crop grass, and with much the same kind of pleasure, had by some happy chance laid hold of some forbidden reading matter, brought in and left there with missionary intent, no doubt, by some Protestant cousin. It fell into the right hands if enjoyment had been its end. The reading matter was ornamented with smudgy illustrations all the more exciting to the little girls because they could not make head or tail of them. The stories were about beautiful but unlucky maidens, who for mysterious reasons had been trapped by nuns and priests in dire collusion; they were forced to take the veil—an appalling rite during which the victims shrieked dreadfully—and condemned forever after to most uncomfortable and disorderly existences. They seemed to divide their time between lying chained in dark cells and assisting other nuns to bury throttled infants under stones in moldering rat-infested dungeons. (193)

In the first draft (leaf 27), Miss Porter had initially written: "During vacation on their grandmother's farm, Maria and Miranda, who read as naturally and constantly as ponies crop grass, and with much the same kind of pleasure, had got hold by some happy chance laid hold of some forbidden reading matter, brought in and left there with missionary intent, no doubt, by some Protestant cousin." Miss Porter had written "got hold," thought again, and deleted the phrase. She then proceeded with "by some happy chance had laid hold of," thus giving the sentence the periodicity it would not have otherwise had. More important, however, is the choice of the more elegant "laid hold of" over "got hold," since this is something like the reverse of the kind of choice she made in letting the simile "as ponies crop grass" stand. The choice of levels of diction is, I suspect, inseparable from the problem of point of view in Miss Porter's work. This problem in "Old Mortality" might be stated as follows: How effectively to direct the reader's apprehension of a completed action involving the growing consciousness of a child, which consciousness must be dramatized as if it were happening in the present moment and appreciated by the mature narrator as family history; all this to be done so as to point to a probable conclusion, one which will satisfy the reader's sense of completeness without giving the game away. Miss Porter's argument at this narrative moment is a modest one but it prepares the reader for the crisis to come in Miranda's renunciation of family and home country. Down to the smallest element of language, the South of the "folks down home" jostles for house room a fabricated, romantic South, a South nourished, as for Miranda and Miss Porter herself, on an early and, for many, a fatal diet of the likes of Poe and Scott. The homely simile works in its aptness first, but it serves also to locate the provincial. The slightly pretentious "laid hold of" makes a claim for a disastrous, unattainable myth, which Miranda will, at least in part, see through.

Sigurd Burckhardt has observed that

> just as the scientist, charged with keeping the material universe intelligible, is, from a common-sense point of view, absurdly sensitive to minute data which call the grand existing order into question, so the poet is inordinately aware of any evidence that human communion-through-language is perhaps only an illusion; that language itself, once it is deprived of its external props, may be merely a vast game of question-begging, in which we presuppose the community we pretend to establish by speaking.[15]

Writing of the history of that language in poetry, he concludes, "For the poet the shift from Divine Providence to actuarial tables is a linguistic one." For Miss Porter, an ironic tension is achieved by the simultaneous blending and playing-off against each other of linguistic levels, an effect which separates both Miss Porter and Miranda from their childhood homes. No less importantly, it separates Miss Porter from Miranda, the fictionalized version of herself.

46

II

The failure of love, that is, the incapacity to imagine fully another's humanity, to act upon such imagination with a degree of generosity, and to abjure that vicious counterfeit of love, sentimentality, is by now so pervasive a theme in modern writing as to be something like a common topic. As treated in *Ship of Fools,* it surprised friends and repelled strangers, but it need not have, since it had its logical antecedent in Miss Porter's earlier work. In "Old Mortality," a bit less satiric in mode than the longer work, somewhat less allegorical in genre but no less ironic in its own way, Miranda, for the moment at least, rejects love outright. For her it comes to that when, her marriage foundering, she accidentally meets in the same compartment Cousin Eva Parrington going home to Cousin Gabriel's funeral. When she sees her father again, she thinks she can abandon the past.

Cousin Eva is such an imposing character, such a strikingly successful characterization that, despite her essential pathos, her forthrightness, and her toughness, as she articulates her own view of the corruption of the society of Miranda's childhood, she could easily mislead the reader into supposing her chic psychologically determined rationale of Amy's career to be Miss Porter's view as well. But the novella is worked out otherwise and Miss Porter will soon have us attuned to this.

Miss Porter has Miranda recall the past of fluttering debutantes and fancy dress balls in a gothic image, provided by Cousin Eva, of smiling, festering female corpses in procession, but she significantly endows Miranda with the capacity to recognize the excessiveness of the image. She has her think, "Of course, it was not like that. This is no more

47

true than what I was told before, it's every bit as romantic."
(216) These last five words are inserted as a revision (leaf
58) in Miss Porter's hand and I take them to be especially
important in the way that they state and arrange the terms
of the thematic conflict in "Old Mortality." Once the modern
historical correction of specious Southern romanticism is
resisted as no less romantic in its own way in how it substi-
tutes one unacceptable myth for another, the question of Miranda's identity at the end of the novella cannot be answered
by simply identifying her as one of the "new women" who
have cast aside a bogus birthright to take their places in the
great, clear-eyed world. The answer, then, must lie elsewhere. Miss Porter's stylistic choice, her decision once
again to be explicit, helped to determine this.

The repudiation, in a series of passages recalling the
conclusion of Joyce's *Portrait*, is like Stephen's, a kind of
non serviam. Miranda will have no more of her American
Southern heritage, a legacy the putative virtue of which she
suspected, in her brightness, even as a child. She thinks of
the mendacity of her romantically self-deluded family and
of the failure of her own marriage. She too, like Cousin Amy,
eloped. " 'I hate love,' she thought, as if this were the answer,
'I hate loving and I hate being loved, I hate it.' " (220–21)
The clause "as if this were the answer" is arresting. It is another insertion (leaf 63), presumably a "correction" made
just before packing the manuscript off to the editors. It is
akin to "Oh, what did grown-up people mean when they
talked, anyway?" in its insistent rhetorical direction toward
the work's encompassing action. Miranda will turn up much
older but only a bit wiser in other guises in *Ship of Fools*.
She will be, even when not explicitly identified as such, the
Catholic *manqué* seeking secular grace, living without philosophical certainty, but *as if* such certainty were accessible,
since there is no other way to live.

Punctuated as it is (there are commas in two places

where normally there would be full stops), the sentence is more an emotional exclamation than an intellectually measured assertion. The effect of the punctuation together with "as if this were the answer," in itself not unlike an old-fashioned authorial intrusion, is to prime us to suspect that not through Miranda's fine consciousness alone will we get the answers to a series of explicit questions around which, as much as by other means, "Old Mortality" gets its thematic consistency. A novella, not an essay, and therefore like a novel in that its agent of imitation is character, "Old Mortality" will not make good on its promises, will not answer its own questions outside the possibilities of character; it does not answer them for Miranda in any decisive way. In the way of the "classical modern" it will answer them for the reader somehow, including by means of style.

Immediately preceding the passage in which Miranda rejects love, there is a crucial one apparently slighted by all commentators:

> . . . all her earliest training had argued that life was a substance, a material to be used, it took shape and direction and meaning only as the possessor guided and worked it; living was a progress of continuous and varied acts of the will directed toward a definite end. She had been assured that there were good and evil ends, one must make a choice. But what was good and what was evil? (220)

This passage follows Miranda's asking herself, "O, what is life . . . and what shall I do with it?" She asks this of herself in "desperate seriousness, in those childish unanswerable words. . . ." She supposes further that her life is "something of her own" and she asks, ". . . what shall I make of it?" There follows then a curious fact: "She did not know that she had asked herself this." The reason "she did not know" is the statement, above, of "her earliest training." Miranda's family is not only of a time and a place but also of a persuasion. They are, as were Miss Porter's, Catholics and it was as such that Miranda was raised and trained, first by her kinfolk and then by the sisters. That life is "a substance, a material to be used," is the formulation of Aquinas making Aristotle acceptable to Christian doctrine.[16] The guiding and the working and the "acts of the will" are the causes in a Christian existentialism, though, significantly, Aquinas would have said not "good and evil ends" but good ends and less good ends. Evil for him is the choice of a less good end once one has the knowledge of the good and the less good. One is struck then by an apparent contradiction: the young Miranda who in desperation repudiates the whole of her past and everyone in it, who denounces the very emotion which makes affection possible, does so automatically out of a sense of unbearable frustration at not knowing how to live a Catholic life; above all, she formulates the question for herself in quasi-Thomist terms but without knowing that she is formulating a question at all, since by now it is her second nature. The meaning, then, is, this: Miss Porter has undercut Miranda and put her at sufficient distance to enable us to see her truly in a way that she cannot see herself. Her sympathies are with the young woman, yes; the case against Miranda's past has been well made, but there is no case to be made against the necessity of second nature and, moreover, Miss Porter does not want to make a case, since that second nature is hers as well as Miranda's. Miranda must try to make something of herself. A heroine of sorts, she will succeed indifferently in no common way and her success will be painful, an action of failure. Her success will be in the honesty of the effort, the struggle to discriminate between the good and the less good; and all around her will be "that majestic failure of man in the western world." [17] Like Joyce, an avowed influence, Miss Porter will hope, without hope, that God will make his appearance to justify the supposition that life has a meaning; meanwhile what choice has one but to proceed without confidence as if it had a meaning, and to be perpetually outraged that the stories of our childhood will not come true? [18] One recalls here Joyce's answer to the question, When did you leave the Catholic Church? "That's for the Church to say." [19]

Nowhere more clearly than in "Old Mortality" can Miss Porter be seen as classical in her formal resolution of the conflict between the subjective person writing and the objective artist. "She has made a story out of her anger," said Eudora Welty, "and if outrage is the emotion she has most strongly expressed, she is using outrage as her cool instrument." [20]

Chapter 3
"Noon Wine," Henry James, and the Novella

Miss Porter's rightful place among the classical moderns—Yeats, Joyce, Pound, Eliot, and James—writers whom she has admired and whom we think of as having in common at least a successful concern with the possibilities of a continually purified English language through a rigorous and, above all, conscious imaginative use—should have been clear from the first with the shorter pieces and certainly with *Ship of Fools;* the latter as we have seen is a work only apparently shaggy and need not have vexed so many commentators. That one who had long respected the fiction of Sterne, especially *Tristram Shandy,* and had translated Lizardi, would write *Ship of Fools,* quite as it was done, was to be expected, despite her intention of making of it a shorter work. A six hundred page "Flowering Judas" was not likely, but critics, ignoring both the power of influences and, for the classical writer, the demanding logic of genre,[1] expected just that.

Miss Porter's avowed affinity with Henry James is decisively formal. In "the master" she saw the triumph of "making," the effective ordering of experience by the means of style. For James, ordering meant a strict limiting (and it is in this sense as well that *he* earns the designation *classical*). In his introduction to *Roderick Hudson* he had declared, "Really, universally, relations stop nowhere, and the exquisite problem of the artist is externally but to draw, by a geometry of his own, the circle within which they shall happily *appear* to do so." In "The Days Before," Miss Porter dilates on this dictum:

William James was fond of a phrase of his philosopher friend Benjamin Paul Blood: "There is no conclusion. What has concluded, that we might conclude in regard to it?" That is all very well for philosophy, and it has within finite limits the sound of truth as well as simple fact—no man has ever seen any relations concluded. Maybe that is why art is so endlessly satisfactory: the artist can choose his relations, and "draw by a geometry of his own, the circle within which they shall happily *appear* to do so." While accomplishing this, one has the illusion that destiny is not absolute, it can be arranged, temporized with, persuaded a little here and there. And once the circle is truly drawn around its contents, it too becomes truth.

Because Henry James often wisely drew his circle small, *Daisy Miller* was not to be *The Portrait of a Lady;* "The Beast in the Jungle" was not to be a novel. Nor, for the same reason, was Miss Porter's "Noon Wine." The metaphor of the circle tells. The romantic writer might fancy himself seeing or singing, but the classical James, and Miss Porter after him, circumscribes.[2]

It was a little disconcerting then to learn of Miss Porter's irritated insistence, soon after the proliferation of bad reviews, that *Ship of Fools* was, indeed, a novel. Her unfriendly critics had called it, among other things, a long tedious short story. I have asked if *Ship of Fools* might not be neither a badly attenuated short story nor a novel. It is a work large in all important ways, and if it is a bad novel, its magnitude must be accounted for by the efficacy of another classification, because, whatever it is, it is a fine and moving fiction. It was equally disconcerting to read in Miss Porter's preface to her *Collected Stories* the following disparagement of genre classification by a scornful blurring of distinctions:

> I beg the reader one gentle favor for which he may be sure of my perpetual gratitude; please do not call my short novels *novelettes*, or even worse, *Novellas.* Novelette is classical usage, for a trivial dime-novel sort of thing; Novella is a slack, boneless,

affected word that we do not need to describe anything. Please call my works by their right names; we have four that cover every division: short stories, long stories, short novels, novels. I now have examples of all four kinds under these headings, and they seem very clear, sufficient and plain English.

For Henry James the novella was "that blessed form." Blackmur writes in his introduction to James's *The Art of the Novel*, "The novella—*the long short story or the short novel* [italics mine]—was perhaps James's favourite form, and the form least likely of appreciation in the Anglo-Saxon reading world, to which it seemed neither one thing nor the other." For Blackmur there is—he supposes incorrectly, I think—less confusion. The novella for him is neither one thing nor another; it is *either* one *or* the other, take your pick. Since presumably, for Blackmur, a long short story becomes a short novel only by changing its name, a short short story would be a novel only by being longer. In any case, even Mr Blackmur, curiously for a Jamesian, does not here subscribe to the Jamesian aesthetic as embodied in the metaphor of the circle. For to see a fiction as one thing or another according to its length is not to draw the circle but to extend the raveling line.

In order to do justice to Miss Porter in her own Jamesian terms, one must arrogate to himself the right to propose that she sells her own work short at times when she elects to function as formal critic, since only in her terms (e.g., designating *Ship of Fools* a novel) can her work be criticized. Similarly "Noon Wine," in my view one of the three or four finest novellas by an American author, would be, by any useful formal definition of a novel, a fatally underfed piece of work.

To choose to leave the furniture undescribed argues thereby for a specific artistic choice and implies that economy in art is a formal feature as well as a virture. Hardly anyone disagrees that *Billy Budd* and *War and Peace* are both war narratives of considerable merit and that *War and Peace* is longer. But it would be incorrect to say that the former is lesser than the latter because it is shorter, or that it is shorter because it is lesser. Amplitude as a characteristic of a work might determine a work's length but amplitude cannot be measured thereby, and insofar as it determines length it might determine length downward. *Oedipus Rex,* one supposes, is great because it has not a bit less plot than it needs; if it had a bit more plot it would be a different action and, I suspect, a lesser one. Melville in effect chose the novella rather than the novel form when he chose not to give us the panoramic sweep of the battlefield but rather to focus on the closeup of the ship. The formal difference between the novella and the short story might be illustrated by supposing that Melville had settled on a narrative in which his protagonist, Billy, would be seen in the context of but one encounter with his antagonist, Claggart. The circumstances of Billy's entry into the life of the ship and the fatal outcome for him of his relationship to its personnel would then have been the broader but merely implied outcome of the events. *Billy Budd* would thus have been a work of different proportions—a short story.

As for the short story, it is not of much help to define it merely as a work longer than an anecdote, shorter than a novella, still shorter than a novel, capable of being read in one sitting, and having a single effect. These are sometimes accurate descriptions but they are not defiinitions. Since the difference between the novella and the novel is largely formal rather than quantitative, there is no reason why, theoretically, although it is practically improbable, a novel could not be a page or two shorter than a long novella, even when set in the same type. By the same token, a tediously long anecdote might well be as long as a short novella. It is difficult to imagine exactly where the short story would fit in this contest of weights and measures. Finally, what any one reader can peruse in one sitting depends only on his anatomy. The short story, then, is likely to be longer than an anecdote and shorter than a novel only because it tries to accomplish different ends. It strives for the development of fewer motifs than the novel, with fewer characters and in less historical time. It therefore requires less narration, less exposition, and no extended denouement; it depends more on the telling gesture and, like the lyric, on evocative diction. Nevertheless, the short story need not be of less magnitude, in Aristotle's terms, than the novel. If *Anna Karenina* is more admirable than Hemingway's "The Killers," it is not simply because the latter is fiction in a shorter form; it is more admirable probably for the same reason that all of Tolstoi's short fiction is more admirable than *The Sun Also Rises.* At its best, the short story implies the universe that the novel describes.

James's "The Lesson of the Master" is a novella and not a long short story, because it is more ambitious than the short story. It introduces more characters, more fictional time, more motifs, more settings, and more revelatory moments than the author of a short story would want. It is not a short novel either. A novel, even of the same length as "The Lesson of the Master," would in all likelihood show the reader how the main characters got that way. St. George's career would be dramatized. Here it is summarized. Why does James summarize St. George's career rather than dramatize it at length over a long period of fictional time? I suppose he does this because St. George's career is important to the work only in two ways: It stands for certain values lost or corrupted and, most crucially, it fatally affects that career or another character.

"Noon Wine" covers only nine years of historical time. The setting is severely limited to the Thompson farm. Side trips, such as Mr. Thompson's to town, are expositional allusions. Even the excruciating and decisive visit to the Mc-

Clellans is recollected from the recent past. Eleven of the work's forty-six pages are devoted to Helton's first day on the Thompson farm, which is hardly the ratio proper to an extended fiction. Most of Helton's nine years are covered by such transitions as "as the seasons passed" and "the years passed." Of Helton's nine years, only the second, with its purchase of the cheese press and the strange incident which "made Mrs. Thompson uneasy," is crucial to the work's end. Almost a full third of the novella is devoted to the Hatch scene, including the killing. Only very slightly less is devoted to the consequences of the killing which deal almost exclusively with Thompson's efforts at self-justification. The entire court trial, a staple of the novelistic treatment, is recollected, not dramatized. Many times the number of words is devoted to a treatment of Thompson's antipathy to certain "womanish" aspects of farming. The Thompson sons, although essential finally, figure slightly except in the crucial "shaking" episode. Little day-to-day action is represented except in terms of Helton's improvement of the farm. Helton is always present in the background. There is no representation of his thoughts, even indirectly, and little speculation about him by the other characters. Finally, Mrs. Thompson herself is hardly internalized.

One can conclude that Miss Porter, by giving a sense of the passage of time without the drama of an extended action, wrote a novella. An extended action is not indicated, according to the fiction's realized intention: Thompson's career consists of the alteration of his material condition, but his character remains the same; the slight events of his life do not effect an outcome; rather they prefigure a catastrophe which, in itself, simply reveals what has all along been the case, namely, that Thompson, in the full pride of a fraudulent masculinity, has throughout been "dead," [3] has worked his wife into her own grave, and has alienated his sons. The work points consistently to a revelation, not a resolution. A full working out of Thompson's fate would have called for the explicit representation of a series of episodes in a cause-and-effect relationship over a period of many more than nine years, perhaps beginning with childhood (or cradling a childhood), showing how Thompson "became." That is, a novel would have been called for. Instead, Thompson is "shown forth" in a terrible reversal of his outward situation at the conclusion of, not as the result of, the events of a relatively few years. Had the same results been effected by merely implying the passage of time, with only the killing of Hatch in the foreground, the fiction would not have been a novella. It would have been a short story. But Miss Porter, to the great advantage of her art, did not choose to draw her Jamesian circle that tightly.

Chapter 4
Lawrence, "María Concepción," and the Feminine

> I found myself asking [of *Lady Chatterley's Lover*] "Why should
> I defend a worthless book just because it has a few dirty words
> in it? Let it disappear of itself and the sooner the better." [1]

In this ruthless and seemingly unfair judgment, there
is something of the quintessential Katherine Anne Porter in
the way that it appears to reduce to a startlingly simple
equation a great deal of complicated argument about literature and censorship. There are similiarly obstinate passages
throughout *The Days Before* and those of us who have
familiarized ourselves with Miss Porter's sentiments, and her
own way of shaping them, were not surprised, for example,
to read that she also agreed with Ford Madox Ford's remark
that "eighty per cent of the people of this world are stuff
to fill graves with." [2] To point out that Stalin might have
said the same thing the day before he died is probably to
miss the point altogether by ignoring the rhetoric and its
context and failing to see above all that Miss Porter's is a
peculiarly feminine mind in the best sense of the word. [3] The
summary evaluation of Lawrence's novel and the apparently
cruel judgment on nearly everyone are both hyperbole in
that they are designed to emphasize, not to deceive. They
are calculated to correct the sentimentalized and conceited
fatuity of too many men with a no-nonsense vision of a hard
reality enjoyed by a great many, if too few, women.

The interviewer had said: "I believe you yourself
said that you felt Scott Fitzgerald was writing about people
who were of no importance." Miss Porter's reply was:

I did. And I still think so. Somebody said I shouldn't feel like that, that everybody was important. Well, that's just one of the fallacies of the world. That's one of the things we say when we think we're being democratic. Eighty per cent of the people of this world, as Ford Madox Ford said, are stuff to fill graves with. The rest are the ones that make it go round. We might as well face that. I was in New York at the time they were having those tea dances and Scott Fitzgerald's romantic dreams about all the collegiate boys and girls dancing in the afternoons of false romance and luxury, and the low sweet fever of love. That sort of thing. And I simply couldn't stand it because I couldn't stand the society of those people. I ran like a deer every time I got near them. And poor Hart [Crane], he came here and said they were just cutting paper dollies. Poor man, what a terrible time we had with him. He was doomed I think. His parasites let him commit suicide. He made such a good show and they had no lives of their own, so they lived vicariously by his, you know. And that of course is the unpardonable sin.[4]

There are two items to remark on in this statement, both of them characteristic of Miss Porter's style of mind. First, she will be damned (I use the word advisedly) if she is going to get down on all fours to explain that she does not mean she is advocating mass extermination of the "worthless" or even that she means the remaining 20 percent are much better ("I am a passenger on that ship," she said of her *Ship of Fools*) or that they too should then be solved finally. The "fallacies of the world" are, for her, fictions we live by and necessarily so, including the one that deems everyone important. We had better try to treat everyone *as if* he were important and we had better do it better than we have ever done, despite the probability that we cannot succeed in so doing any more spectacularly in the future than we have in the past. The failure of love in the modern world is for her disappointing enough but what is truly outrageous is the effort to both obscure it and atone for it by a spurious humanitarianism which here she calls "being democratic." Second, inherent in her hyperbolic phrases is a pure anger. It is directed at those who expect her to appreciate the shallow and the trivial. For Miss Porter they consitute a genuine threat, since shallowness and triviality can, in the persons of their bearers, altogether do one in. The unpardonable sin, for Miss Porter as it was for Henry James, is parasitism. Living off another's moral or intellectual capital is, after all, not robbery but murder.

Her view of Lawrence as a "faulty" [5] writer is only partly an expression of the artist who is annoyed with herself at having neglected her work to enlist in futile social causes. She found the defense of Lawrence's book against censorship to be after all extra-literary, an expression of a spurious self-congratulatory liberalism in the cause of bad writing. She is said to have told Archer Winsten years before (1937) that she was "afraid for her mental freedom," and would therefore not embrace Marxism although she was attracted to it. Why, she wanted to know, should she have rebelled in her youth against the Jesuits only to take another yoke now? Above all, though, her concern is with the language and it is because of this concern that she could become so exercised at the claptrap, as she saw it, which characterized the efforts of critics to justify, on aesthetic grounds, Lawrence's use of explicit sexuality and taboo four-letter words. Miss Porter never went in for either. "Yet," she insists,

> the language needs those words, they have a definite use and value and they should not be used carelessly or imprecisely. My contention is that obscenity is real, is necessary as expression, a safety valve against the almost intolerable pressures and strains of relationship between men and women, and not only between men and women but between any human being and his unmanageable world. If we distort, warp, abuse this language which is the seamy side of the noble language of religion and love, indeed the necessary defensive expression of insult towards the sexual partner and contempt and even hatred of the insoluble stubborn mystery of sex itself which causes us such fleeting joy and such

61

cureless suffering, what have we left for a way of expressing the luxury of obscenity which, for an enormous majority of men, by their own testimony, is half the pleasure of the sexual act?

I would not object, then, to D. H. Lawrence's obscenity if it were really that. I object to his misuse and perversions of obscenity, his wrong-headed denial of its true nature and meaning. Instead of writing straight, healthy obscenity, he makes it sickly sentimental, embarrassingly so, and I find that obscene sentimentality is as hard to bear as any other kind. I object to this pious attempt to purify and canonise obscenity, to castrate the Roaring Boy, to take the low comedy out of sex. We cannot and should not try to hallow these words because they are not hallowed and were never meant to be. The attempt to make pure, tender, sensitive, washed-in-the-blood-of-the-lamb words out of words whose whole intention, function, place in our language is meant to be exactly the opposite is sentimentality, and of a very low order. Our language is rich and full and I daresay there is a word to express every shade of meaning and feeling a human being is capable of, if we are not too lazy to look for it; or if we do not substitute one word for another, such as calling a nasty word—meant to be nasty, we need it that way—"pure," and a pure word "nasty." This is an unpardonable tampering with definitions, and, in Lawrence, I think it comes of a very deep-grained fear and distrust of sex itself; he was never easy on that subject, could not come to terms with it for anything. Perhaps it was a long hang-over from his childish Chapel piety, a violent revulsion from the inane gibberish of some of the hymns.

[Lawrence's] first encounter with dirty words, as he knew them to be, must have brought a shocking sense of guilt, especially as they no doubt gave him great secret pleasure; and to the end of his life he was engaged in the hopeless attempt to wash away that sense of guilt by denying the reality of its cause. He never arrived at the sunny truth so fearlessly acknowledged by Yeats, that "Love has pitched his mansion in the place of excrement"; but Yeats had already learned, long before in his own experience that love has many mansions and only one of them is pitched there—a very important one that should be lived in very boldly and in hot blood at its own right seasons; but to deny its nature is to vulgarise it indeed. My own belief in this, that anything at all a man and woman wish to do or say in their sexual relations, their love-making, or call it what you please, is exactly their own business and nobody else's. But let them keep it to themselves unless they wish to appear ridiculous at best, at worst debased and even criminal. For sex resembles many other acts which may in themselves be harmless, yet when committed in certain circumstances may be not only a sin, but a crime against human life itself, human feelings, human rights—I do not say against ethics, morality, sense of honour (in a discussion of the motives not of the author perhaps, but of the characters in this novel, such words are nearly meaningless), but a never-ending wrong against those elements in the human imagination which were capable of such concepts in the first place. If they need the violent stimulation of obscene acrobatics, ugly words, pornographic pictures, or even low music—there is a negro jazz trumpeter who blows, it is said, a famous aphrodisiac noise—I can think of no argument against it, unless it might be thought a pity their nervous systems are so benumbed they need to be jolted and shocked into pleasure. Sex shouldn't be that kind of hard work, nor should it, as this book promises, lead to such a dull future.[6]

It is interesting to compare Lawrence's treatment of the sexual with Miss Porter's as it is found in "María Concepción," that astounding first effort, a fabulous tale on which it is no stricture to say she never improved.

Granted the vastly different context, the following notoriously "arcadian" scene from *Lady Chatterley's Lover* has the look, at least, of a similar scene in "María Concepción."

"Do you know what I thought?" she said suddenly. "It suddenly came to me. You are the 'Knight of the Burning Pestle!' "

"Ay! And you? Are the Lady of the Red-Hot Mortar?"

"Yes!" she said. "Yes! You're Sir Pestle and I'm Lady Mortar."

"All right, then I'm knighted. John Thomas is Sir John, to your Lady Jane."

"Yes! John Thomas is knighted! I'm my-lady-maiden-hair, and you must have flowers too. Yes!"

She threaded two pink campions in the bush of red-gold hair above his penis.

"There!" she said. "Charming! Charming! Sir John!"

And she pushed a bit of forget-me-not in the dark hair of his breast.

"And you won't forget me *there*, will you?" she kissed him on the breast, and made two bits of forget-me-not lodge one over each nipple, kissing him again.

"Make a calendar of me!" he said. He laughed and the flowers shook from his breast.

"Wait a bit!" he said.

He rose, and opened the door of the hut. Flossie, lying in the porch, got up and looked at him.

"Ay, it's me!" he said.

The rain had ceased. There was a wet, heavy perfumed stillness. Evening was approaching.

He went out and down the little path in the opposite direction from the riding. Connie watched his thin, white figure, and it looked to her like a ghost, an apparition moving away from her.

When she could see it no more, her heart sank. She stood in the door of the hut, with a blanket round her, looking into the drenched motionless silence.

But he was coming back, trotting strangely, and carrying flowers. She was a little afraid of him, as if he were not quite human. And when he came near, his eyes looked into hers, but she could not understand the meaning.

He had brought columbines and campions, and new-mown-hay, and oak-tufts and honeysuckle in small bud. He fastened fluffy young oak-sprays round her breasts, sticking in tufts of bluebells and campion: and in her navel he poised a pink campion flower, and in her maiden-hair were forget-me-nots and woodruff.

"That's you in all your glory!" he said. "Lady Jane, at her wedding with John Thomas."

And he stuck flowers in the hair of his own body, and wound a bit of creeping-jenny round his penis, and stuck a single bell of a hyacinth in his navel. She watched him with amusement, his odd intentness. And she pushed a campion flower in his moustache, where it stuck dangling under his nose.

"This is John Thomas marryin' Lady Jane," he said. "An' we mun let Constance an' Oliver go their ways. Maybe—"

He spread out his hand with a gesture, and then he sneezed, sneezing away the flowers from his nose and his navel. He sneezed again.

"Maybe what?" she said, waiting for him to go on.

"Eh?" he said.

"Maybe what? Go on with what you were going to say," she insisted.

"Ay, what *was* I going to say?"

He had forgotten. And it was one of the disappointments of her life, that he never finished.

A yellow ray of sun shone over the trees.[7]

It was Lawrence's hope that with such writing he could employ the explicit to transform the prurient into the innocent, and succeeded, in the view of Miss Porter and a few others, only in the unintentionally comic, the making of doleful farce. The weakness of the scene is precisely in the explicitness, both Lawrence's and his characters'. Their extremely self-conscious eroticism Lawrence takes quite as seriously as they do, and but for certain accidents of birth Mellors and Connie could exchange sexes and be hoking a haggis without seriously reducing the already fundamentally sexless feeling of the scene.

When María Concepción comes upon Maria Rosa and her own husband, the unfaithful Juan, she thinks:

"So Maria Rosa has a man!" María Concepción stopped short, smiling, shifted her burden slightly, and bent forward shading her eyes to see more clearly through the spaces of the hedge.

Maria Rosa ran, dodging between beehives, parting two stunted jasmine bushes as she came, lifting her knees in swift leaps, looking over her shoulder and laughing in a quivering, excited way. A heavy jar, swung to her wrist by the handle, knocked against her thighs as she ran. Her toes pushed up sudden spurts of dust, her half-raveled braids showered around her shoulders in long crinkled wisps.

Juan Villegas ran after her, also laughing strangely, his teeth set, both rows gleaming behind the small soft black beard growing sparsely on his lips, his chin, leaving his brown cheeks girl-smooth. When he seized her, he clenched so hard her chemise gave way and ripped from her shoulder. She stopped laughing at this, pushed him away and stood silent, trying to pull up the torn sleeve with one hand. Her pointed chin and dark red mouth moved in an uncertain way, as if she wished to laugh again; her long black lashes flickered with the quick-moving lights in her hidden eyes.

65

María Concepción did not stir nor breathe for some seconds. Her forehead was cold, and yet boiling water seemed to be pouring slowly along her spine. An unaccountable pain was in her knees, as if they were broken. She was afraid Juan and Maria Rosa would feel her eyes fixed upon them and would find her there, unable to move, spying upon them. But they did not pass beyond the enclosure, nor even glance towards the gap in the wall opening upon the road.

Juan lifted one of Maria Rosa's loosened braids and slapped her neck with it playfully. She smiled softly, consentingly. Together they moved back through the hives of honeycomb. Maria Rosa balanced her jar on one hip and swung her long full petticoats with every step. Juan flourished his wide hat back and forth, walking proudly as a game-cock.

María Concepción came out of the heavy cloud which enwrapped her head and bound her throat, and found herself walking onward, keeping the road without knowing it, feeling her way delicately, her ears strumming as if all Maria Rosa's bees had hived in them. Her careful sense of duty kept her moving toward the buried city where Juan's chief, the American archaeologist, was taking his midday rest, waiting for his food.

Juan and Maria Rosa! She burned all over now, as if a layer of tiny fig-cactus bristles, as cruel as spun glass, had crawled under her skin. She wished to sit down quietly and wait for her death, but not until she had cut the throats of her man and that girl who were laughing and kissing under the cornstalks. (5–6)

Later, having killed Maria Rosa:

María Concepción stood in the doorway, looming colossally tall to his betrayed eyes. She was talking quickly, and calling his name. Then he saw her clearly.

"God's name!" said Juan, frozen to the marrow, "here I am facing my death!" for the long knife she wore habitually at her belt was in her hand. But instead, she threw it away, clear from her, and got down on her knees, crawling toward him as he had seen her crawl many times toward the shrine at Guadalupe Villa. He watched her approach with such horror that the hair of his head seemed to be lifting itself away from him. Falling forward upon her face, she huddled over him, lips moving in a ghostly whisper. Her words became clear, and Juan understood them all.

For a second he could not move nor speak. Then he took her head between both his hands, and supported her in this way, saying swiftly, anxiously reassuring, almost in a babble:

"Oh, thou poor creature! Oh, madwoman! Oh, my María Concepción, unfortunate! Listen. . . . Don't be afraid. Listen to me! I will hide thee away, I thy own man will protect thee! Quiet! Not a sound!"

Trying to collect himself, he held her and cursed under his breath for a few moments in the gathering darkness. María Concepción bent over, face almost on the ground, her feet folded under her, as if she would hide behind him. For the first time in his life Juan was aware of danger. This was danger. (14)

The self-conscious pastoral playfulness which Lawrence expected us to find sublime in his scene, Miss Porter found only preposterous. For her, passionate relationships between men and women are not to be rendered in fiction as utopian. A debt to their seriousness must be paid in blood. After all, are we not flesh *and* blood, and is it not in the bloodiness of sexual love exactly where much of its disturbing mystery lies?

Much of the power of Miss Porter's scene is in the fact of its being a painful kind of tableau. We regard Maria Rosa playing the coy nymph but from the point of view of María Concepción whose murderous feelings correct the possibility of conventional erotic romanticism. We hold our breath with her. We do not palpitate with her enemy. Within, the image of Maria Rosa's fully draped thighs "knocked" by the heavy jar at her wrist is fundamentally steamier than anything comparable and unclad in Lawrence's novel, but it is also terrible both in its moment and in the larger context of the story, first, because of its pathos and, second, because it carries the burden of violence and dread so carefully promised us at the outset:

María Concepción walked carefully, keeping to the middle of the white dusty road, where the maguey thorns and the treacherous curved spines of organ cactus had not gathered so profusely. She would have enjoyed resting for a moment in the dark shade by the roadside, but she had no time to waste drawing cactus needles from her feet. Juan and his chief would be waiting for their food in the damp trenches of the buried city.

She carried about a dozen living fowls slung over her right shoulder, their feet fastened together. Half of them fell upon the flat of her back, the balance dangled uneasily over her breast. They wriggled their benumbed and swollen legs against her neck, they twisted their stupefied eyes and peered into her face inquiringly. She did not see them or think of them. Her left arm was tired with the weight of the food basket, and she was hungry after her long morning's work.

Her straight back outlined itself strongly under her clean bright blue cotton rebozo. Instinctive serenity softened her black eyes, shaped like almonds, set far apart, and tilted a bit endwise. She walked with the free, natural, guarded ease of the primitive woman carrying an unborn child. The shape of her body was easy, the swelling life was not a distortion, but the right inevitable proportions of a woman. She was entirely contented. Her husband was at work and she was on her way to market to sell her fowls.

Her small house sat half-way up a shallow hill, under a clump of pepper-trees, a wall of organ cactus enclosing it on the side nearest to the road. (14)

The image of María Concepción as the very type of unevolved femaleness, as much *of* the earth as *on* it, carrying within her the future of race and sex, is couched in brutal terms, not the brutality of an overwrought society turned in on its darker self but the brutality of original conflict. She gives only passing attention equally to the cruel thorns of nature piercing her flesh, to the incipient life within her, and to mindless nature, stupid, but alive around her neck. Soon she will slaughter those fowls with as little self-consciousness as she will later murder the other Maria. A woman lives in the world's way. Juan can romanticize himself as the revolutionary, but María Concepción knows herself better.

It was the earlier D. H. Lawrence of *Sons and Lovers*

who pleased Miss Porter, and if the contrasted scenes illustrate a difference between the romantic Lawrence and the classical Porter it is in this more traditional novel that we can see something of an affinity, if not an influence. With a great uncommon sense, Julian Moynahan noted of *Sons and Lovers:*

> These scenes and expository passages, in which characters act out their vital destinies, sometimes mislead critics on the prowl for symbolism into supposing they were planted in the narration as "keys" to hidden meaning. But in the sense that symbols always point beyond themselves to something buried, there is little symbolism in *Sons and Lovers.* Early in the novel Miriam is shown afraid to "let herself go" fast and high when she is taking turns with Paul on the barn swing. Later on, she cannot let herself go in her sexual experiences with Paul. The first situation is not meant to adumbrate the second. Both are equally real and final as revelations of Miriam's diminished vitality, her tendency to shrink back from life, whether she is making love, feeding chickens, trying to cope with Mrs. Morel's dislike of her, or merely looking at flowers.[8]

María Concepción's sexual vitality like Miriam's want of it similarly is not "symbolized." In that brilliant opening view of María there is no metaphorical configuration of sexuality nor is there a promise of an eroticism to come. The view we get of María is as literal and uninterpretable as our first view of Odysseus, stripped and stranded, the very embodiment of the idea of man as male, neither less nor more so for his nakedness. His "sexiness" was established long before a nymph was introduced into the narrative by Homer's depiction of a careless piratical nature and a decisively unfeminine yen for immortality through fame. Our first sight of her gives us María Concepción's immortality as located in her womb, a gracefulness which, judging from her walk, she takes easily as her due. This is how it begins. As an end she will kill a woman for a child she feels to be her own. Before that she will butcher a goose so men may eat.

69

Chapter 5
Symbolism, the Short Story, and "Flowering Judas"

If one opens Jean Stafford's *Collected Stories* [1] to, say, "The Lippia Lawn," which begins, "Although its roots are clever, the trailing arbutus at Deer Lick had been wrenched out by the hogs," he is promised the work of a poet, and this promise the other stories generally keep. It is the "clever," employed for all its worth, including *its* root sense, that does it almost all, and this is as it should be if, as I suppose with a few others, the short story is, in crucial ways, most like the lyric in that its agent is neither plot nor character, but diction. When its language is felicitous, decorous, and evocative, the tone and feeling will cradle characterization, enhance idea, and imply action which the novel must nearly always dramatize or fail. But this is not to say that the short story *is* a poem and here, too, is where many fledgling writers and not a few experienced critics have gone wrong.

The short story is not quite a poem any more than it is a short novel boiled conveniently down to bite size. So it cannot, therefore, be done with sounds, sights, and symbols alone. Surely he was correct who contended that "the storyteller must have a story to tell, not merely some sweet prose to take out for a walk." And so was that editor who wrote to Katherine Anne Porter, "No plot, my dear, no story," [2] although how he supposed that stricture to apply to *her* work I can imagine only in a way that does him no credit.

Commentators and editors have grouped Miss Porter's stories in a variety of ways: early—late, Miranda—

Laura, new order—old order, and Mexican—non-Mexican,[3] to name a few. This habit is conventional and usually harmless enough; it does not mislead if one keeps in mind that it is usually more a descriptive than a critical practice. It is more to the point of criticism, however, to see a "story" as falling naturally into two groups which are explicitly evaluative according to degree of formal accomplishment: realized stories with sufficient verbal efficacy to compensate adequately for the absence of the explicit causal-temporal logic essential only to most longer fictional forms; and alleged stories which no amount of verbal magic can rescue from a poverty of implied plot and other indispensable narrative features.

"During the 1940's, it was as symbolist that Miss Porter was most effusively praised by totemist critics," James William Johnson reminds us. "In fact, criticism of her work became tantamount to an intellectual parlor game: 'Let's see who can find the most abstruse symbols in "Flowering Judas."' Her work survived this craze, which was largely unnecessary, since the truth is that her symbols operate on the most direct level and, where she intends a multiplicity of meaning, Miss Porter almost always tells the reader so."[4] It ought to be added to Mr. Johnson's refreshingly commonsensical observation that although her work has survived "this craze," the "craze" itself dies hard. The neo-euhemerism of the thirties and forties seems down but by no means out, and the readings of "Flowering Judas" which can serve as paradigms of that era's notorious and, often, hilarious symbol-mongering have, to my knowledge, never been recanted. Moreover, the epigones of the totemists are still publishing critiques of Miss Porter's stories founded on the assumption that there is nothing, given sufficient ingenuity, that cannot be read as metaphysical verse.[5]

"Flowering Judas" is, to be sure, a highly figurative composition. The modern short story almost invariably is,

71

because, perhaps paradoxically, its author is likely to write in a realistic mode. For whereas the publicly verifiable in the novel requires extended treatment, partly in order to represent time sequentially, the familiar in the short story, dealing as it does with the moment, can be represented best by a good deal of shorthand. The result has been a "symbolic realism" where the most ordinary events are imitated, but by a selective process so scrupulous as to evoke at least what the novel might show or tell. When most successful, as in "Flowering Judas," the evocations are practically symbolic in that they stand for more than themselves. It follows that, mistaking the means for the end, the amateur is forever producing the unwritten. In the place of the authentic story there is fobbed off something between an impressionistic hodgepodge and a bastard lyric, known at times as the "mood piece" and at others as the "prose poem." There is also the "slice-of-life," and, more recently, the "open-ended" story, a legitimate enough form, if it is not open at both ends, top and bottom. Since on the contrary "Flowering Judas" is so plainly a fully realized effort to tell a tale classically, that is, to move a serious theme through implied time by means of characters who act on ethical choices, and to do this, moreover, without failing to accommodate to theme, wherever possible, the details of image and fable, it might, therefore, be wise to be a bit warier than most critics have been of reading this story as if its meaning partook of its figuration rather than, as I believe to be the case, the reverse.

There has been no slackening of published interest in "Flowering Judas," but the standard reading continues to be the West-Stallman analysis which appeared in a college anthology of short fiction in 1949.[6] I know of no reading that does not take off from it, at least in its basic assumption of the accessibility of theme and meaning through symbolism. The text is incorrectly titled "The Flowering Judas." If one believed that the causes of error are unconscious but real, the accident would be seen as a true mistake. For West and Stallman, *the* flowering Judas is virtually *the* story. The analysis itself is titled "Theme through Symbol," which, I contend, is not a viable concept for narrative fiction. The West-Stallman reading asks what the purpose of the individual symbol is, and replies that it is to "signify the theme." "In the title itself" the "most important" symbol "occurs," and the source is given as Eliot's ' 'Gerontion." "This is scarcely a coincidence," we are told, "since Eliot's passage so clearly suggests Laura's activity at the end of the story." The five lines in which the words "flowering Judas" appear are quoted as if they are proof. The Judas tree is seen quite simply as "a symbol for the betrayer of Christ." Laura's eating the buds is a "sacrament . . . of betrayal." If we put aside the question of failure to cite evidence of Miss Porter's specific debt to Eliot in this instance, we are nonetheless free to grant her known interest in Eliot and the obviousness of the betrayal theme in both poem and story do, admittedly, constitute presumptive evidence of source. But to go further in lining up the story with the poem is to jump to conclusions about the use of the symbol, based mistakenly on the assumption that symbols are used in stories quite as they might be in poems, that is, to signify theme. In fact, in Miss Porter's story, the symbol of the flowering Judas is employed to enhance theme and finally to reiterate theme, but not to be a sign of theme as if theme had not been established by other means. Laura is found wanting from beginning to end, and the meaning of the story does not wait on a final symbolic revelation to make accessible what would otherwise be mysterious. "I have a great deal of religious symbolism in my stories," Miss Porter recently allowed, "because I have a very deep sense of religion and also I have a religious training. And I suppose you don't invent symbolism. You don't say, 'I'm going to have the flowering Judas tree stand for

betrayal,' but of course it does." [7] Of course, it does, because
given the association of the name Judas it can. But it does
only if the author, in effect, employs it to that end. If the
reader can recognize the Judas tree as a symbol of betrayal,
he can do so legitimately, and not arbitrarily, only if he has
been permitted to see betrayal in the story's action. It is the
story, all in all, that makes of this particular tree a working
symbol of anything whatever. In a work as psychologically
realistic [8] as this one, concerned as it is with the levels of
a young woman's harassed consciousness (Laura's mind is in
fact the work's arena), the Judas tree does not stand primarily and independently as the figure of pagan treachery,
analogous to Laura's treachery. Rather it illuminates, dream
image that it is, the natural depths of the bedeviled feelings
of a woman who cannot, when awake, come to terms with
those feelings. Seen this way, "Flowering Judas" is not a
symbolic story in the sense that it depends on symbols to
pull its thematic irons out of the fire. The entire work is in
a way "symbolic" insofar as it impels the reader to attend to
one striking detail and not another. But within this sense of
symbol the Judas tree as a figure is not the most important.
It cannot, logically, be more important than any other narrative detail which gives us insight into Laura's character. It
may seem crucial because of its strategic location, that is,
at the end. Thus placed, however, it can astonish only a
reader who has paid little attention to the work's beginning,
as might astonish the figurative phrase "my eyes burned" at
the conclusion of Joyce's "Araby," a story which begins,
"North Richmond Street, being blind, was a quiet
street. . . ."

Miss Porter has written of "Flowering Judas":

> All the characters and episodes are based on real persons and
> events, but naturally, as my memory worked upon them and time
> passed, all assumed different shapes and colors, formed gradually
> around a central idea, that of self-delusion, the order and meaning
> of the episodes changed, and became in a word fiction.

74

The idea first came to me one evening when going to visit the girl I call Laura in the story, I passed the open window of her living room on my way to the door, through the small patio which is one of the scenes in the story. I had a brief glimpse of her sitting with an open book in her lap, but not reading, with a fixed look of pained melancholy and confusion in her face. The fat man I call Braggioni was playing the guitar and singing to her.

In that glimpse, no more than a flash, I thought I understood, or perceived, for the first time, *the desperate complications of her mind* and feelings, and I knew a story; perhaps not her true story, not even the real story of the whole situation, but all the same a story that seemed *symbolic truth* to me. If I had not seen her face at the very moment, I should never have written just this story because I should not have known it to write.[9] [Italics mine]

"Flowering Judas" owes its greatness not at all to some opportunistic employment of a conventional religious symbol to signify theme but to a brilliant narrative practice throughout, one capable of representing a feeling that, once apprehended by the reader, permits him to see with what overriding intelligence Miss Porter knew her Laura, "the desperate complication of her mind" and what it meant.

The celebrated dream sequence on which the story ends and which is supposed to be central in its resolution and revelation through the symbol of the tree and the buds follows:

The tolling of the midnight bell is a signal, but what does it mean? Get up, Laura, and follow me: come out of your sleep, out of your bed, out of this strange house. What are you doing in this house? Without a word, without fear she rose and reached for Eugenio's hand, but he eluded her with a sharp, sly smile and drifted away. This is not all, you shall see—Murderer, he said, follow me, I will show you a new country, but it is far away and we must hurry. No, said Laura, not unless you take my hand, no; and she clung first to the stair rail and then to the topmost branch of the Judas tree that bent down slowly and set her upon the earth, and then to the rocky ledge of a cliff, and then to the jagged wave of a sea that was not water but a desert of crumbling stone. Where are you taking me, she asked in wonder but without fear. To death, and it is a long way off, and we must hurry, said Eugenio. No, said Laura, not unless you take my hand. Then eat these flowers, poor prisoner, said Eugenio in a voice of pity, take and eat: and from the Judas tree he stripped the warm bleeding flowers, and held them to her lips. She saw that his hand was fleshless, a cluster of small white petrified branches, and his eye sockets were without light, but she ate the flowers greedily for they satisfied both hunger and thirst. Murderer! said Eugenio, and Cannibal! This is my body and my blood. Laura cried No! and at the sound of her own voice, she awoke trembling, and was afraid to sleep again. (102)

It has been prepared for by a single reference to the Judas tree earlier in connection with a "brown, shock-haired youth" who pleaded for her love in vain. Laura, for her part, "could think of nothing to do about it."

The sense one gets of Laura's emotional stinginess is not so much that, Judas-like, she has betrayed the young man in withholding human warmth but that, like the central figure of "Theft," Miss Porter's story of another young woman who is seen explicitly to have stolen life's spiritual riches from *herself,* Laura has betrayed Laura. We know next to nothing of the young man, but we know how desperately Laura needs to fulfill herself. The young man will fare badly, but it is not inevitable. Laura, on the other hand, is doomed forever to suffer her own starving soul, a fact confirmed by a negation and fear of life and truth, the note on which the very last image is played out. But nothing of what is given to the reader anywhere in the dream sequence is unprepared for, and is, moreover, explicitly *reasoned* by the narrator the moment it is possible to intrude sufficiently to explain Laura. In a work of fiction in which the narrator tells the reader what he needs to know, no symbol so arbitrary as to liken a frightened nunlike girl to the historical Judas is artistically allowable. Nor is Miss Porter guilty of such faulty aesthetic judgment.

If Miss Porter is a symbolist only in the sense we have described, that is, as a writer whose choices of vocabulary, of levels of diction, and of varieties of image work insistently to induce one to read beyond mere denotation, she is also a symbolist in "Flowering Judas" in the sense of her own phrase "symbolic truth," which I take to be synonymous with "meaning."

Finally, the West-Stallman reading has it that

> Laura is not redeemed, even though she desires it, as the eating of the buds of the Judas tree suggests. Her sacrament is a devouring gesture and Eugenio calls her a cannibal, because she is devouring him (Man). She is, like Judas, the betrayer—the destroyer; and her betrayal, like his, consisted in an inability to believe. Without faith she is incapable of passion, thence of love, finally of life itself.
>
> This is the "moral" of the story, translated as it is into the language of Christian theology: "Man cannot live by bread alone." Distilled even beyond that, into the language of statement, we might say that the theme is this: "Man cannot live if he accepts only materialistic values"; or, to put it into a positive statement: "Only in faith and love can man live." This does not, however, represent the "meaning," for the meaning is, as we have said, the total embodiment—the form. The statement is only an inadequate attempt on the part of the reader to seek out the author's intention. The question the student should ask next is, "How much does it leave unsaid?" (291)

It is a little like shoveling sand in a windstorm to so much as begin to take issue with this crowd of New Critical pieties: the historical Christian assumptions as the ground for reading a "moral" statement; the fudging of the question of meaning by equating it simply with "form"; and the raising of the old specter of "intention." Miss Porter makes it quite clear that her intention is to elucidate the "desperate complications of her [the protagonist's] mind" and that the "meaning" of the story is in whatever general human nature can be discerned from such an elucidation. The "symbolic truth" Miss Porter speaks of is precisely in the way Laura's career corresponds to the ambiguous and paradoxical condition of recognizable modern man. Laura "is not at home in the world." In this configuration the most crucial fictional device is not the Judas tree but Laura herself. The theme, then, can hardly be stated as "man cannot live if he accepts only materialistic values." "Flowering Judas" dramatizes nothing so much as the fact that modern man, especially modern political man (Braggioni), lives and thrives, but more like a pig than a human. As for Laura, who has been enlisted in Braggioni's cause, she is so far from being materialistic that, in her "notorious virginity," she has even disowned her body. She is the most spiritual of women, but her spirit has been given over to a crusade founded not on a faith in the soul of man or the love of God but on the mindless force of history. In surrendering herself thus, she has surrendered everything.

If one must state a theme, it would be that of *self*-betrayal, and, more interestingly for a fictional construct, the way in which anomic modern life can be made of it.

> But she cannot help feeling that she has been betrayed irreparably by the disunion between her way of living and her feeling of what life should be, and at times she is almost contented to rest in this sense of grievance as a private store of consolation. Sometimes she wishes to run away, but she stays. (91–92)

In their haste to see the meaning of "Flowering Judas" as inhering in its "most important" symbol, as it "occurs," commentators after the New Critics have failed consistently to distinguish the foreground of the narration from its shadowy, memorial background, where a series of rather theoretical and underdramatized "betrayed" characters have compromised Laura's Mexican life. Even Braggioni, despite his imminence and despite his taking part in the most affecting of scenes (his homecoming), curiously resides as almost exclusively an evil presence in Laura's desolate consciousness. There is, in fact, only one character upstage, Miss Porter's thrillingly intelligent narrative voice, guiding us over the landscape of Laura's mind, making sense for us of its "disunion." This she does in the historical present, so that the truth may be held up for inspection in life's continual moment.

Chapter 6
People Who Cannot Speak
for Themselves

I

Of her last published short work to date, Miss Porter wrote:

"Holiday" represents one of my prolonged struggles, not with questions of form or style, but my own moral and emotional collision with a human situation I was too young to cope with at the time it occurred; yet the story haunted me for years and I made three separate versions, and with a certain spot in all three where the thing went off the track. So I put it away and it disappeared also, and I forgot it. It rose from one of my boxes of papers, after a quarter of a century, and I sat down in great excitement to read all three versions. I saw at once that the first was the right one, and as for the vexing question which had stopped me short long ago, it had in the course of living settled itself so slowly and deeply and secretly I wondered why I had ever been distressed by it. I changed one short paragraph and a line or two at the end and it was done.[1]

That the "struggle" was worth it is plain. In its own way "Holiday" is quite as successful as the shorter "He," and the novella, "Noon Wine," both of which it resembles in some important ways, especially, in its devastating effect on the reader's sense of that lonely, vain, and painful labor which is life itself, but also in the brilliant and poignant depiction of characters who are more or less dumb and who, precisely because of their inarticulateness, are made to serve the author's purpose of inducing a more articulate character, with whom the reader can identify, to experience a revision of life.

"Holiday" is *about* the Müllers, German farmers residing in East Texas, but it is *within* and treats *of* the mind of a young nameless woman-narrator who, in her concerns and the feelings with which she voices them, bears a strong resemblance to the Miranda of "Pale Horse, Pale Rider" as well as the Miranda of "Old Mortality." The Müllers, as surely and colorfully drawn as Flaubert's peasants in early scenes of *Madame Bovary*, are, nevertheless, practically faceless, since by their physically healthy animal mindlessness they are virtually indistinguishable from each other and so remain at a distance from the reader, thus permitting them to stand perfectly for that mass of undifferentiated humanity of which we are all a part and from which we are, paradoxically, distinct. They are the cast on the stage of the narrator's troubled consciousness.

Ottilie, the forgotten sister consigned to the family role of kitchen servant, being incapable of speech, can only try to indicate to the narrator, in agonizing little scenes, the turbulence in her heart. There are thus two dramas being enacted at once: the play of life-and-death in the family story and the education of the narrator as she perceives Ottilie's astonishing role in that story. It is the narrator's career which is central, and the difficulty for the reader is that he is enjoined, as in a Henry James fiction, to stay with the author's subtle intelligence as it backs and fills, progressively correcting faulty impressions, ultimately drawing truthful conclusions about the unalterable laws of human existence from a welter of tangled appearances. Miss Porter keeps nothing from the reader but she stops just the crucial millimeter short of doing the reader's decisive work.

The opening paragraph of "Holiday" is of considerable importance to the story and notable as fiction.

At that time I was too young for some of the troubles I was having, and I had not yet learned what to do with them. It no longer can matter what kind of troubles they were, or what finally became of them. It seemed to me then there was nothing to do but run away from them, though all my tradition, background, and training had taught me unanswerably that no one except a coward ever runs away from anything. What nonsense! They should have taught me the difference between courage and foolhardiness, instead of leaving me to find out for myself. I learned finally that if I still had the sense I was born with, I would take off like a deer [2] at the first warning of certain dangers. But this story I am about to tell you happened before this great truth impressed itself upon me —that we do not run from the troubles and dangers that are truly ours, and it is better to learn what they are earlier than later, and if we don't run from the others, we are fools. (407)

Unlike that kind of contemporary writer who claims narrative effacement as an exclusive virtue and is in fact, one suspects, too timid to state his work's meaning lest the work fail to live up to the auctorial promise, Miss Porter states that meaning in "Holiday" in a secondary but explicit way as "this great truth," and in an equally explicit but primary way, since it has now been dramatized, at the conclusion:

Well, we were both equally the fools of life, equally fellow fugitives from death. We could celebrate our good luck, we would have a little stolen holiday. . . . (435)

The delight in the work is to experience the less explicit, often exquisitely subtle, always ironical, movement of concrete iteration to reiteration, until the terms "fools of life" and "fellow fugitives from death" are known for what they can mean beyond abstraction, through the narrator's experience of the wordless girl. This narrator, "too young" to put her "troubles" in philosophical perspective, enjoys a series of illuminations in moments of fictional time which will ripen from meaning to significance in the story's encompassing action, the years one can assume to have followed the end of the action proper. From the position of maturity, the narrator can *tell* "this story" in a locus of wisdom, but in so doing she will let it unfold couching it in images of nature, at a Jamesian pace, that is, at a speed consistent with experience itself, so that for the reader it will be psychologically dramatic.

A friend and former schoolmate, knowing as little as we do of the young woman's "troubles"—only that she wants a holiday by herself—urges her to lodge with the Müllers.

> Louise had then—she still has—something near to genius for making improbable persons, places, and situations sound attractive. She told amusing stories that did not turn grim on you until a little while later, when by chance you saw and heard for yourself. So with this story. Everything was just as Louise had said, if you like, and everything was, at the same time, quite different. (407–08)

There is a touch of resentment against Louise, reminiscent of Miranda's against her family in "Old Mortality," people who do you wrong by making you the victim of their own romanticism, a fundamentally untruthful view of life founded on an inability to separate appearance from reality. Describing the Müllers' ménage in paradisiac terms, Louise concludes, "I was there in the summer when the peaches and watermelons were in." (408) But she is cut short with "This is the end of March," thus drawing the line between a springtime revision of the past and a view of the same objective situation as a wintry present reality.

Louise had spoken of "endless daughters and sons and sons-in-law and fat babies falling about the place; and fat puppies. . . ." (408) There were "cows, calves, and sheep and lambs and goats and turkeys and guineas roaming up and down the shallow green hills, ducks and geese on the ponds." (408) The cataloguing of animal nature, so vital, and for Louise so arcadian, is for the narrator a presentiment of its opposite. Louise had said that her "favorite" was "a darling little black thing named Kuno . . . ," (408) who materializes in fact as "an enormous black dog of the detestable German shepherd breed" and who menaces the narrator the moment she reaches the farm, confirming her conviction that "in daily life . . . there are also such useful things as plain facts that should be stuck to through thick and thin." (409) But more importantly there is notice in this seemingly slight incident, and in its gross animal image, of the cruel fact of passage in all created life and, for one who senses it, the fear of inevitable death. Later for the narrator there is a satisfaction as well in coming to terms with death and the fear of it. It is crucial to the story in the way that it justifies the young woman's presence thematically and does so, in part, through the dog, Kuno, as he is reintroduced, now in connection with Ottilie, to invoke the theme of nature, dumb but strenuous and striving. The occasion is the death of Mother Müller, the story's turning point:

> On that day I realized, for the first time, not death, but the terror of dying. When they took the coffin out to the little country hearse and I saw that the procession was about to form, I went to my room and lay down. Staring at the ceiling, I heard and felt the ominous order and purpose in the movements and sounds below—the creaking harness and hoofbeats and grating wheels, the muted grave voices—and it was as if my blood fainted and receded with fright, while my mind stayed wide awake to receive the awful impress. Yet when I knew they were leaving the yard, the terror began to leave me. As the sounds receded, I lay there not thinking, not feeling, in a mere drowse of relief and weariness.
>
> Through my half-sleep I heard the howling of a dog. It seemed to be a dream, and I was troubled to awaken. I dreamed that Kuno was caught in the trap; then I thought he was really caught, it was no dream and I must wake, because there was no one but me to let him out. I came broad awake, the cry rushed upon me like a wind, and it was not the howl of a dog. I ran downstairs and looked into Gretchen's room. She was curled up around her baby, and they were both asleep. I ran to the kitchen.

Ottilie was sitting in her broken chair with her feet on the edge of the open oven, where the heat had died away. Her hands hung at her sides, the fingers crooked into the palm; her head lay back on her shoulders, and she howled with a great wrench of her body, an upward reach of the neck, without tears. At sight of me she got up and came over to me and laid her head on my breast, and her hands dangled forward a moment. Shuddering, she babbled and howled and waved her arms in a frenzy through the open window over the stripped branches of the orchard toward the lane where the procession had straightened out into formal order. I took hold of her arms where the unnaturally corded muscles clenched and strained under her coarse sleeves; I led her out to the steps and left her sitting there, her head wagging. (433)

Her own terror having receded with the departure of the funeral party, the young woman, supposing that Ottilie is wretched at having once again been left behind, bundles her into a battered wagon and tries to overtake the train.

Ottilie, now silent, was doubled upon herself, slipping loosely on the edge of the seat. I caught hold of her stout belt with my free hand, and my fingers slipped between her clothes and bare flesh, ribbed and gaunt and dry against my knuckles. My sense of her realness, her humanity, this shattered being that was a woman, was so shocking to me that a howl as *doglike* and despairing as her own rose in me unuttered and died again, to be a perpetual ghost. (Italics mine; 434)

The configuration is thus rounded out: nature, human and general, is denied a romantic possibility as in the perpetual passing hour of death; men howl in concert, but each for his own life. This paradox, bodied forth here in the narrator's experience of Ottilie's very flesh, is earlier merely stated: "I could do nothing but promise myself that I would forget her, too; and to remember her the rest of my life." (427)

When she arrives at the farm, burdened with her own sorrow, the young woman sees only "scanty leafless woods," and, as if speaking more of her own life as she had found it, reflects that "there was nothing beautiful in these woods now except the promise of spring, for I detested bleakness, but it gave me pleasure to think that beyond this there might be something beautiful in its own being, a river shaped and contained by its banks, or a field stripped down to its true meaning, ploughed and ready for the seed." (410) A child will be born to one of Ottilie's sisters, as easily as a foal is dropped, but the narrator is "passionately occupied with looking for signs of spring." (419) Amid the search for a comfortable sign of life, one which will bear on the narrator's personal distress, Ottilie makes known to the young woman her true identity. She is more than an idiotic kitchen slave; she is a member of the family, everyone's flesh and blood. She is Ottilie and she knows it, and she would have another know it. She shows the narrator a childhood photograph of herself, once a lovely child, a duplicate in appearance of her sisters and brothers:

> The bit of cardboard connected her at once somehow to the world of human beings I knew; for an instant some *filament* lighter than cobweb spun itself out between that living center in her and in me, *a filament from some center that held us all bound to our unescapable common source,* so that her life and mine were kin, even a part of each other, and the painfulness and strangeness of her vanished. She knew well that she had been Ottilie, with those steady legs and watching eyes, and she was Ottilie still within herself. For a moment, being alive, she knew she suffered, for she stood and shook with silent crying, smearing away her tears with the open palm of her hand. Even while her cheeks were wet, her face changed. Her eyes cleared and fixed themselves upon that point in space which seemed for her to contain her unaccountable and terrible troubles. She turned her head as if she had heard a voice and disappeared in her staggering run into the kitchen, leaving the drawer open and the photograph face downward on the chest. (Italics mine; 426)

If it is the image of the puppy Kuno become a howling dog that, for the narrator, connects Ottilie with herself, time, and nature, it is the filament which is the image of nature connecting everything with everything. In selecting for her figure from nature that slenderest of threads which supports the pollen-bearing organ of the flower, Miss Porter made at once the most apt and ironical choice.

"Holiday" ends with the astonishing sight of Ottilie, moments before so wretched, now "happy and gay," on the way to her mother's funeral. For her it is a rare day off; she is alive in the moment, with "the hot sun on her back," and the narrator ponders her own "ironical mistake," which is not merely that of failing initially to understand that Ottilie was at once close to her and beyond reach as fellow "fool" and "fellow fugitive from death," but it is also the mistake we can see working back through the story to the beginning, where the narrator supposes that she could "send [Louise] word now and then if anything interesting was happening." (407) The narrative form of "Holiday" argues for specific varieties of communicable understanding, from which Louise is excluded because she is confirmed in her own view of reality for which the Müller farm stands, and because she exists in time simultaneously with the narrator as the "too young" fictional character, not with the narrator as story-teller old enough to have reflected on the truth of the fiction. As a fictional character Louise cannot see what is "interesting" in the young woman's experience as interest is made of abstracting the true from the "real." Finally, given her own way with words, Louise's articulateness stands between her and the narrator. Ottilie's muteness, however, allows for communion.

II

There is no more harrowing story in English than Miss Porter's "He," a little gem of enormous thematic magnitude. A masterpiece of compression, a universe of human suffering is worked out in its nine pages in a way that involves the reader most painfully, without resorting to sentimentality or preachment; yet its moral implications are weighty, and although Miss Porter succeeds as always in maintaining that "delicate balance of rival considerations," [3] the ethical demands on the reader are such as to make him take sides. In this instance Miss Porter's method is Joycean. There seems to be no narrator at all. The voice we hear is a removed one, giving us, for the most part, an "objective" representation of events reflected through the minds of the characters, not apparently through the mind of the author. Yet the choice of detail and the manner of representation are consistently, until the end, ironic, thus constituting an auctorial commentary of the most devastating sort.

> Mrs. Whipple loved her second son, the simple-minded one, better than she loved the other two children put together. She was forever saying so, and when she talked with certain of her neighbors, she would even throw in her husband and her mother for good measure. (49)

We are put on notice that, no matter how His mother feels about Him, that feeling is bound to be something less than or other than a superabundance of unalloyed love, just as in "Clay" we know that no matter how she feels about the laundry, poor old Maria, unable to admit it, especially to herself, does not "like" the place at all:

> After the break-up at home the boys had got her that position in the *Dublin by Lamplight* laundry, and she liked it. She used to have such a bad opinion of Protestants but now she thought they were very nice people, a little quiet and serious, but still very nice people to live with. Then she had her plants in the conservatory and she liked looking after them. She had lovely ferns and wax-plants and, whenever anyone came to visit her, she always gave the visitor one or two slips from her conservatory. There was one thing she didn't like and that was the tracts on the walls; but the matron was such a nice person to deal with, so genteel. [4]

With Mrs. Whipple as with Maria, we are given, seemingly, only her sentiments indirectly, but in a way to make them ring false in their self-delusion. Both women protest too much, but their protestations of "loving" and "liking" are stated less as expository facts than as qualities of their minds. Miss Porter does not write, "Mrs. Whipple was forever saying she loved her second son, the simple-minded one, better than she loved the other two children put together." Nor does Joyce write that "Maria kept insisting that she liked the laundry, her life there, and the people in it." Mrs. Whipple's "love" for her son, as Maria's satisfaction with life at the laundry, are stated as facts, as the two characters see the facts. The vocabulary of Maria's view of the laundry is her own, and the repeated use of "like" has the quality of her own discourse. Mrs. Whipple's "forever saying so" is a fact about her that Mrs. Whipple herself would have gladly asserted.

In this way Miss Porter adapts to her own ends the modern practice of putting the action at such a distance as to suggest that it is transpiring, like life itself, without benefit of an author the reader knows very well to be there. However, there is no confusion in her own particular use of this method between narrative distance and moral distance. There is everywhere evident in the story an awareness on her part of the putative quality of a highly selective realism. "He" is the work of an author relentlessly directing the reader how and what to think without appearing to do so.

Mrs. Whipple's overwhelming concern for the appearances of her life leads one immediately to look for the realities. These realities are so appalling that, as the story ends with the child being taken away, one finds himself seated with the neighbor, "driving very fast, not daring to look behind him."

> He sat there blinking and blinking. He worked His hands out and began rubbing His nose with His knuckles, and then with the end

of the blanket. Mrs. Whipple couldn't believe what she saw; He was scrubbing away big tears that rolled out of the corners of His eyes. He shriveled and made a gulping noise. Mrs. Whipple kept saying, "Oh, honey, you don't feel so bad, do you? You don't feel so bad, do you? for He seemed to be accusing her of something. (58)

The scene is heartbreaking in its pathos but, the complexities of the human condition having been so forcefully arrayed, we sense that the driver's fear of looking back is more than an avoidance of emotional pain occasioned by a spectacle of acute sadness. "Behind him" is what is behind everyone, a career of human error, human imperception, human deficiency in the face of the human demands on us for generosity, even when, having received little, we have little to give.

Mrs. Whipple, like Royal Earle Thompson, cares above all for two things, a life free of tribulation and the good opinion of others. The first is the case, as for the central character of "Noon Wine," because life has given her nothing but woe; the second, again as it is for Mr. Thompson, because of a nagging sense of her own very limited worth in the face of deprivation. (Unlike the Whipples' farm, the Thompson farm flourishes, but no thanks to Mr. Thompson, whose distress lies finally in a feeling of true superfluousness.) A sentimentalist and a hypocrite, there is nothing about Mrs. Whipple for us to like but everything for us to take seriously, for although it is clear that Miss Porter would have had her treat Him differently, the burden of the story is the terrible question of how many of us could have succeeded in giving love where Mrs. Whipple failed. It is easy enough for the reader to see Mrs. Whipple's failure for what it is, an incapacity to recognize Him as a person despite his animal dumbness, a capacity which the narrator of "Holiday" has in abundance in respect to Ottilie. But Miss

Porter permits the reader to judge not the person but only the human proclivity.

III

> Mr. Helton's silence, the pallor of his eyebrows and hair, his long, glum jaw and eyes that refused to see anything, even the work under his hands, had grown perfectly familiar to the Thompsons. At first, Mrs. Thompson complained a little. "It's like sitting down at the table with a disembodied spirit," she said. "You'd think he'd find something to say, sooner or later."
>
> "Let him alone," said Mr. Thompson. "When he gets ready to talk, he'll talk."
>
> The years passed, and Mr. Helton never got ready to talk. (236)

All one knows about the taciturn Olaf Helton is that he can, as if an agent of mysterious natural forces, turn the Thompson farm into a flourishing garden; he plays the same doleful tune, year after year, on one of his precious harmonicas; and he is capable of violence. The origins and details of his past life come to us only through the word of the diabolical Homer T. Hatch, who has come to hunt him down:

> "What did he do?" asked Mr. Thompson, feeling very uneasy again.
>
> "Oh, nothin' to speak of," said Mr. Hatch, jovially, "jus' went loony one day in the hayfield and shoved a pitchfork right square through his brother, when they was makin' hay." (251)

We distrust Hatch's every word, but we recall that Helton had manhandled the Thompson children when he discovered that they had tampered with his harmonicas.

> "Brother was going to get married," said Mr. Hatch; "used to go courtin' his girl nights. Borrowed Mr. Helton's harmonica to give

her a serenade one evenin', and lost it. Brand new harmonica."
(251)

Mr. Hatch then explains that Mr. Helton killed his
brother because he would not buy him a harmonica to re-
place the one he lost; Mr. Helton was then put away for a
"loonatic" and later escaped. As for the song Mr. Helton
plays:

> "One of those Scandahoovians told me what it meant, that's how
> I come to know," said Mr. Hatch. "Especially that part about get-
> ting so gay you jus' go ahead and drink up all the likker you got on
> hand before noon. It seems like up in them Swede countries a man
> carries a bottle of wine around with him as a matter of course, at
> least that's the way I understood it. Those fellers will tell you any-
> thing, though—" He broke off and spat. (252)

Now we trust Hatch's information because Hatch does not.

Helton's very wordlessness encourages speculation
but obviates the possibility of a satisfactory answer much
beyond his formal relationship with the Thompson family.
He is an imminent presence, but only occasionally palpable.
In the radical sense he is a "literary" character, contrived,
unfamiliar, a felicitous invention, less true to life than to
life's meaning. "Noon Wine" is Mr. Thompson's story but
not without Olaf Helton, who means quite literally both life
and death to him and who, during those long prosperous
years when he silently carries the farm on his shoulders
alone, hovers about Mr. Thompson's conscience, making him
murderously uneasy.

For both Mr. Thompson and Olaf Helton, life is too
much, but it is not at all the same life. If we cannot know
certainly the whole of Helton's story, we can make inferences about it from the awful certainty of Mr. Thompson's
life, and in so doing know Thompson better.

Mr. Thompson, assertive only in his insistence on
doing only a man's work (milking is woman's work), does

poorly even a "man's" work and asserts himself only twice, once when he kills Hatch and once when he kills himself. He recalls the pallid Mr. Whipple who, when the painful moment arrives for taking Him away, says to his wife, "You'll be all right, I guess I'll stay behind. . . . It don't look like everybody ought to leave the place at once." (58) A great rationalizer and self-excuser, Mr. Thompson cannot at last rationalize or excuse away the fates of Hatch and Helton, not only because he knows in his heart his degree of responsibility for another man's death but because he is confronted at last with the blinding sight of his own deficiency as he has experienced it all along at Helton's expense. Mr. Hatch comes to take what is left of Helton's life, which is nothing, having been lived out "before noon," long before his materializing from nowhere one day to bring the inexorable into Mr. Thompson's pathetic career. Olaf Helton is all along the ghost of a young man who had, unlike Mr. Thompson, once "lived."

Royal Earle Thompson talks, therefore he is. Almost without exception his speeches are two-thirds prattle. He says what need not be said or what should not be said.

> He sat on the steps, shot his quid into the grass, and said, "Set down. Maybe we can make a deal. I been kinda lookin' round for somebody. I had two niggers but they got into a cutting scrape up the creek last week, one of 'em dead now and the other in the hoosegow at Cold Springs. Neither one of 'em worth killing, come right down to it. So it looks like I'd better get somebody. Where'd you work last?"
> "North Dakota, . . ."
> "North Dakota," said Mr. Thompson. . . . "That's a right smart distance off, seems to me." (223)

In contrast, Helton's laconic replies have a seasoned grace. He would have Mr. Thompson leave off talking so that he can get to work, but the reader can hear in the man's chattering the violent sound of future doom. No sooner does

Helton start in on his first day's chores than Mr. Thompson heads for town, to return later full of boozey, loquacious "good will." Helton, who when drunk had taken his brother's life, is never seen to drink. Tipsy, Mr. Thompson gives voice to adolescent prurience. Helton had wanted to court a girl in love. Mr. Thompson will try to explain himself to the day he dies, but Helton's death is the last reproach of silence.

Chapter 7
Charles Upton and the Premonition
of Disaster

Commentators, looking back at "The Leaning Tower," a novella published in 1941 about the Germany of a decade earlier, see it as one of Miss Porter's less successful efforts,[1] especially when they compare it unfavorably with her other work, a profitable critical habit perhaps for the biographer but a somewhat meaningless one, in most cases, for others. As I have contended earlier, it is rather unfair to an author, and quite irrelevant to the idea of critical judgment, to hold him to a perennially uniform practice, as if he were not considering literature but the menu in a cafeteria. I think it would be more useful to ask if "The Leaning Tower" is not a successful work on its own terms, and to look further perhaps into the ways in which those terms have not always been clear to everyone.

For Ray B. West, in "The Leaning Tower" Miss Porter's "sensitivity appears to have failed her."[2] The work is not considerable for much of its own, but is "remarkable primarily for its difference from the stories that had come before." The symbolism is heavy-handed (unlike that of "Flowering Judas"), the characters "wooden" (unlike those of "Noon Wine"). The mind through whose consciousness the events are recorded is "inadequate." The explanation is that "perhaps" the pressure of the times "clouded (if not falsified) memories of the original events," as if for West Miss Porter had written not fiction but autobiography, and the proper tools of critical measurement were not therefore primarily aesthetic but historiographic and psychologic.

William L. Nance tells us that the story is defective in many ways:

> Dramatically it is loose, with several barren sketches of discussion, and contains suggestions of the travelogue. During the discussion of world affairs the language sometimes becomes formalized at the expense of verisimilitude and dramatic force, and the entire story suffers from a lack of humor. The Berliners are repeatedly portrayed as pig-like, malicious and sentimental. Charles sketches many of them, emphasizing their unpleasant features; his suspicion that he is a caricaturist may be applied to the author as well. Her efforts to convey the impression of repulsiveness and evil portent cost too much in terms of realism. The leaning tower symbol is another defect; it is insufficiently integrated with its surroundings to represent them effectively, and excessive discussion and explanation of it dim the aura of mystery and suggestiveness which a symbol should possess. The meaning of the symbol is explored most thoroughly in the short closing scene in which Charles returns to his room drunk and sees it repaired, in the corner cabinet, now protected from him by glass. The fragile tower is intended to represent the precarious German culture, once nearly destroyed by a crude America.[3]

Nance concludes with a stricture much like Daniel Curley's [4] on *Ship of Fools:*

> It would seem that in "The Leaning Tower" Miss Porter has entrusted the creative act too extensively to the abstract intelligence, too little to that deep, inner way of working which has proved her only avenue to artistic success.

The price of "abstract intelligence," it seems, is "an overly ambitious semi-allegorical purpose." Most of Nance's objections are not worth our concern; since so many other critics have dwelled on it, however, the question of the tower symbolism is worth our concern.

If the tower is too blatant a symbol, it is curious that critics cannot agree on what it symbolizes. If it all-too-clearly represents for Nance "the precarious German culture, once nearly destroyed by a crude America," it all-too-clearly represents for West "the futile attempts of man to hold onto memories and dreams. . . ." Mooney sees the tower as embodying the "social and political evil" of Nazism. Kendrick sees the tower as "a fitting symbol of a society soon to topple again," thus disagreeing with Nance insofar as "society" and "culture" are not at all synonymous.

It would seem, then, that the symbol is actually mysterious enough to suit even Nance if he only knew it, but in fact the "aura of mystery" surrounding any given symbol can never be dense enough for some critics who rely on it to keep literature up for grabs. In any case, I think it can probably be demonstrated that an interpretation of "The Leaning Tower" depends no more on its symbolism (employed effectively enough, in my view) than does an interpretation of "Flowering Judas." The tower symbol, one supposes, means everything Miss Porter decently says it does and, because it is a symbol, it means something more. But since it is through Charles Upton's experience of Rosa Reichl's Germany that we have any sense of the symbol at all, critics have more properly fretted the question of his adequacy as a central intelligence. However, I think it can also be shown that Upton is not an "inadequate" consciousness but inadequate only enough to permit the reader to participate in the experience at Charles's side without losing patience with his limitations. As such he might well be the envy of any writer of fiction concerned with the nice problems of establishing narrative authority.

Leon Edel, writing of *The Ambassadors*, reminds us of "James's mature belief that life is a process of *seeing*, and through awareness the attaining of understanding." [5] A very inexperienced young man, Charles Upton is, in his artist's view of the world, a male version of Miranda who in turn, we have seen, is a persona for the author herself. His limitations are plain enough but entirely to the point of the story. Quite properly, "He felt young, ignorant, he had so much to learn he hardly knew where to begin." (459) His greenness is the given without which a painfully acquired knowledge of Europe could not be written as a process of experience. An ineffectual kind of ambassador by circumstance of youth, he is also, however, a pictorial artist by profession. As the latter, he is nothing if not a sharply focused eye. If he is also an American and therefore subject to hurt feelings and disappointment in defeated post-World War I Germany, he is as well Miss Porter's means of getting a perspective on her own German experience several years after it. There is much that Charles cannot understand, but what he does not understand is not quite what the story is about. It is more about what he does understand, which is altogether in the realm of feeling and, in the light of history, monumental: first, "a most awful premonition of disaster" (488) and, then, "what he had never known before, an infernal desolation of the spirit, the chill and knowledge of death in him." (495) He is, at the last, a good deal less a naive boy from Texas and more a man of a world about to go up in flames in his sure knowledge, instinctively inferred, that he can do nothing about the awful imminent future. His inferences are objectified in the view of Germany in caricature with which the author provides him; and caricature, by definition, is a distortion and exaggeration in the interest of some truth. Thus the meaning, and significance of the story as well, will intersect and become manifest at the point where we are directed to see that the distortion of the reality of Germany is itself the overriding objective reality of the time of Charles Upton, and hence our own.

Charles can sound downright boobish as when, sitting around with his "friends" discussing the possibility of another world war, he says, ". . . good old sea power. I bet on that. It wins in the long run." (487) Charles knows as little about history as he knows about life, and even less, of course, about what that war on which he is so fatuously speculating will mean to other human beings. But it is not what Charles says or even, at first, what he feels that gives his mind its authority for the reader. It is what he sees and the way he sees it in its graphic peculiarity.

We know that Aschenbach is a writer of the first rank not because Mann's narrator says so in speaking of his reputation but because it is established in "Death in Venice" that Aschenbach writes like Mann, and we have Mann's work before us by which to judge. Similarly, we know that Charles Upton will one day be as good a pictorial artist as Miss Porter is a writer because his way of seeing Germany in its strikingly figurative grotesqueness is hers, insisted on in "The Leaning Tower" and repeated in *Ship of Fools*. The purest anger with which Charles sees his Germans and the near-viciousness with which he represents them in his sketchbook bespeak a callow and uncertain young man taking the hostile way of the world personally; but his hard core is as decent as his eye is keen, and in this latter day we can see his position as frightfully dangerous, his fear as therefore justified, and his juvenile malice natural to a creature truly threatened by death.

Charles is introduced to us as a young man of a self-generating romantic disposition. His boyhood friend, who had visited Germany often, had only said that the streets of Berlin were "polished like a table top," but "Charles saw it as a great shimmering city of castles towering in misty light." He was later to wonder in bitterness how he had "got such an image." (439) The image would change drastically from the medieval heroic to the contemporary swinish:

> He would wander on, and the thicker the crowd in which he found himself, the more alien he felt himself to be. He had watched a group of middle-aged men and women who were gathered in silence before two adjoining windows, gazing silently at displays of

toy pigs and sugar pigs. These persons were all strangely of a kind, and strangely the most prevalent type. The streets were full of them —enormous waddling women with short legs and ill-humored faces, and round-headed men with great rolls of fat across the backs of their necks, who seemed to support their swollen bellies with an effort that drew their shoulders forward. Nearly all of them were leading their slender, overbred, short-legged dogs in pairs on fancy leashes. The dogs wore their winter clothes: wool sweaters, fur ruffs, and fleece-lined rubber boots. The creatures whined and complained and shivered, and their owners lifted them up tenderly to show them the pigs.

In one window there were sausages, hams, bacon, small pink chops; all pig, real pig, fresh, smoked, salted, baked, roasted, pickled, spiced, and jellied. In the other were dainty artificial pigs, almond paste pigs, pink sugar chops, chocolate sausages, tiny hams and bacons of melting cream streaked and colored to the very life. Among the tinsel and lace paper, at the back were still other kinds of pigs: plush pigs, black velvet pigs, spotted cotton pigs, metal and wooden mechanical pigs, all with frolicsome curled tails and appealing infant faces.

With their nervous dogs wailing in their arms, the people, shameless mounds of fat, stood in a trance of pig worship, gazing with eyes damp with admiration and appetite. They resembled the most unkind caricatures of themselves, but they were the very kind of people that Holbein and Dürer and Urs Graf had drawn, too: not vaguely, but positively like, their late-medieval faces full of hallucinated malice and a kind of sluggish but intense cruelty that worked its way up from their depths slowly through the layers of helpless gluttonous fat. (442–43)

Miss Porter's habit of allegorizing evil as a pig-like German who has become a caricature of himself has in it a measure of simple xenophobia as well as a larger measure of artistic felicity, but it serves in "The Leaning Tower" less to limn German nature than to depict human nature at its worst, when its worst manifests itself in brutality and self-pity as the consequence of hardship. Charles Upton can always go home. The Germans *are* home, and home is a battered, demoralized land of the hungry and the hysterical.

Prize fighters got cauliflower ears, but not purposely. It was a hazard of the game. Waiters got something called kidney feet. Glass blowers blow their cheeks all out of shape, so they hang like bags. Violinists sometimes get abscesses on their jaws where they hold the violin. Soldiers now and then have their faces blown off and have to get them put back by surgery. All kinds of things happen to men in the course of their jobs, accidents or just deformities that come on so gradually they are hardly noticed until it is too late to do much about it. Dueling had been a respectable old custom almost everywhere, but there had to be a quarrel first. He had seen his great-grandfather's dueling pistols, the family pride in a velvet-lined case. But what *kind* of man would stand up in cold blood and let another man split his face to the teeth just for the hell of it? And then ever after to wear the wound with that look of self-satisfaction, with everybody knowing how he had got it? And you were supposed to admire him for that. Charles had liked Hans on sight, but there was something he wouldn't know about him if they both lived for a thousand years; it was something you were, or were not, and Charles rejected that wound, the reason why it existed, and everything that made it possible, then and there, simply because *there were no conditions for acceptance in his mind.* (Italics mine; 465)

It is not to Charles's credit that "there were no conditions for acceptance in his mind," since acceptance, in the abstract, is a virtue, but the import of the passage rests not only in its locating the limits of Charles's imagination but in its feeling of desperation, perplexity, and hopelessness. In his naïve way the American must reject the German, and the German in his own way has earned the rejection.

An artist, Charles needs light, and has a right to it. A Texan and young, he needs to go home and grow up. Growing up means to see and accept in sadness the world as it appallingly is. Here the Texan and the artist are one:

The long nights oppressed him with unreasonable premonitions of danger. The darkness closed over the strange city like the great fist of an enemy who had survived in full strength, a voiceless monster from a prehuman, older and colder and grimmer time of the world.

101

"It is just because I was born in a sunny place and took the summer for granted," he told himself, but that did not explain why he could not endure with patience, even enjoy, even look upon as something new and memorable to see, unfamiliar weather in a foreign climate. Of course it was not the weather. (457)

Of course not. It is the climate of life before the disaster; but all premonitions are unreasonable, including those which tell us truthfully to run for our lives.

"It cannot be replaced," says his landlady when Charles destroys her small plaster replica of the Leaning Tower of Pisa. Charles is humiliated, and his impulse is to leave this setting forever.

"It is not your fault, but mine," said the landlady, "I should never have left it here for—" She stopped short, and walked away carrying the paper in her two cupped hands. For barbarians, for outlandish crude persons who have no respect for precious things, her face and voice said all too clearly.

Charles, red and frowning, moved warily around the furniture towards the windows. A bad start, a very bad start indeed. The double panes were closed tightly, the radiator cast an even warmth through the whole room. He drew the lace curtains and saw, in the refracted pallor of the midmorning, winter light, a dozen infant-sized pottery cupids, gross, squat limbed, wanton in posture and vulgarly pink, with scarlet feet and cheeks and backsides, engaged in what appeared to be a perpetual scramble to avoid falling off the steep roof of a house across the street. Charles observed grimly their realistic toe holds among the slate, their clutching fat hands, their imbecile grins. In pouring rain, he thought, they must keep up their senseless play. In snow, their noses would be completely buried. Their behinds were natural victims to the winter winds. And to think that whoever had put them there had meant them to be oh, so whimsical and so amusing, year in, year out. He clutched his hat and overcoat with a wild impulse to slip out quietly and disappear. Maybe he wouldn't come back at all. (447)

In this scene, where Charles Upton is seen for everything he is—young, American, artist, anathema to the superior German, puzzled, intimidated, and homesick—the much worried symbol gets Miss Porter's most careful and extended treatment. It seems less a symbol in the sense of sign-as-metaphor to make concrete some universal abstraction than a way of making vivid, as a grace note, the identity of Charles Upton who should have left on the spot but could not.

"The Leaning Tower," no less than *Ship of Fools*, is painful to read because of its subject. It is nonetheless a joy to see Miss Porter at once containing and illuminating her anger and her disappointment at "this majestic and terrible failure of the life of man in the Western world."

Chapter 1

1. "*Ship of Fools* and the Critics," by Theodore Solotaroff, in *Commentary* 34 (Oct. 1962): 277–86.
2. "Yes, But Are They Really Novels," *Yale Review* 51, no. 4 (Summer 1962): 632–34.
3. Katherine Anne Porter, *Ship of Fools* (Boston: Little, Brown and Company, 1962). Subsequent references are to the same edition and are indicated by page number in parentheses.
4. No claim is made that *Ship of Fools* satisfies this definition of an apologue down to the last painstaking detail, as does *Rasselas* or *Candide;* rather it satisfies the definition in the larger, decisive ways, and, above all, it does so more closely than it satisfies Sacks's or anyone else's definition of a novel.
5. From "A Prologue to the *Ship of Fools,*" trans. Edwin H. Zeydel (New York: Dover Publications, Inc., 1944), pp. 57–58.
6. "Katherine Anne Porter's *Ship of Fools,* a Masterpiece Manqué," *UKCR* 33 (1965): 151–57.
7. Porter, *Ship of Fools,* pp. 264–66.
8. Since Miss Porter has acknowledged her debt to Sebastian Brant, it is appropriate to speak of an echo of *Das Narrenschiff:*

> Who would give gifts in spirit mellow
> Must laugh and be a jolly fellow
> And not say: "I regret my deed,"
> If gratitude and love he'd need. (Chap. 96)

9. There is precedent in Miss Porter's work in the use of this device: In "Old Mortality" where it is employed similarly, "Harry and Mariana, in conventional disguise of romance, irreproachably be-

trothed, safe in their happiness, were waltzing slowly to their favorite song, the melancholy farewell of the Moorish King on leaving Granada." Later, Amy, anything but irreproachable or safe, writes from New Orleans after marrying Gabriel, "we are having a lovely visit. I'm going to put on a domino and take to the streets with Gabriel sometime during Mardi Gras."

10. From a letter to Edward Schwartz, February 20, 1952, in Schwartz, "Katherine Anne Porter: A Critical Bibliography," with an introduction by Robert Penn Warren. *BNYPL* 17 (May 1953): 211–47.

11. In a letter to me, dated March 25, 1967, Miss Porter concurs with this reading of *Ship of Fools* as I contended for it in "The Responsibility of the Novelist: The Critical Reception of *Ship of Fools*," *Criticism* 8 (1966): 377–88. (She does not address herself to the theoretical assumptions, however, on which the reading is based.) In the same letter, Miss Porter contrasts it with "the many dreadful interpretations."

The following from *Harper's,* September 1965, too, supports the supposition that Miss Porter's nominal intention was to write a "novel," but that her inclinations led her elsewhere:

> And then I came to the really tough one, which I called *Ship of Fools,* based on my voyage from Veracruz to Bremerhaven, my first voyage to Europe. Would you believe it wouldn't accommodate itself. I couldn't do it in 25,000 words. And I said I'm not going to do anything more. This is my limit. I'm a short-story writer, and if I can't say what I've got to say in 25,000 words, I won't begin. And this kept haunting me and bedeviled me and I kept writing and taking notes and thinking about it— how to get this into 25,000 words. And it would not. It just obstinately would not. I finally just kept writing and writing. Years passed and I'd go back and add some more and then I'd worry about this thing. I couldn't get rid of it. It had to be written and I had to find a way to write it. And I couldn't, because I was obstinate, you see. I would not write a novel. They'd been after me to write a novel for years. I kept telling them, "I will not— you have to leave me alone. This is my way of working and I am not going to do anything to change it." It was partly obstinacy, partly professional pride, partly the fact that I thought I knew what I could do and what I couldn't do. And I had to work it out. It took me years and years. I'd go back and add

again, and I'd go back over it, and little by little it shaped itself in my mind.

12. *Ship of Fools* is set in 1931. The passengers of the *Vera* sail on August 22 from Veracruz and arrive at Bremerhaven twenty-seven days later, on September 17, after covering an itinerary which corresponds very closely to the actual. The intransigent captain is plainly the type of Captain Thiele.

13. *The Waves* was published in 1931.

14. This review of a work on Mexico by Stuart Chase seems not to have been published. Miss Porter's tone did not suit the *New Republic*, of which Mr. Cowley was book editor from 1929 to 1940.

15. Beggars, vicious or maimed, are powerful images in the depiction of Veracruz in the opening scenes of *Ship of Fools*. The maimed beggar is a Brant figure, dealt with in *Das Narrenschiff*, chap. 63.

   Since Mrs. Treadwell, attacked by a beggar in Veracruz, is one of the more apparent personae for the author, it is interesting to note how Miss Porter opposes the beggar to the artist. The following is a journal account put down in Basel, November, 1932 and published in J. Laughlin, ed. *New Directions in Prose and Poetry* (Norfolk, Conn.: New Directions, 1940), p. 199.

> Worked this afternoon on some notes for *Noon Wine*. The cold darkness is down once more, the beggar's grind-organ is still whining the same miserable tune over and over; it has been whining since early this morning with hardly a pause. The beggar is very fat, with a bald, scaly head; an ill humored looking fellow. His flesh sags on him like dirty rags, and he has trespassed on that curve in the bridge, (the Rheinbrucke) where the artist goes to repaint, by the changing lights and colors of weather and time of day and season, his one theme: the Munster. I have seen this painting change from lush greens and harrowing pinks to morbid purple, to pallid tans and mud tints and swooning grays in the course of these five months in Basel. Yesterday, he went as usual, to set up his easel, and there stood the fat beggar, scowling and twisting the mean tune out of his barrel organ. He did not give way an inch, so the painter edged around him, set up his canvas stool, seated himself, thumb in palette, raised his arm and began grandiosely to sweep the brush over the canvas. Every time the beggar's arm turned with the crank of the barrel organ, he would jog the painter,

and the painter would squirm, but nothing more happened. I decided, then, the beggar should never have another pfennig from me if he loses a hundred pounds from starvation. The painter worked there patiently for an hour, shabby and thin and hungry looking—more than ever so, compared to the fat-jowled beggar. . . .

Next day. The painter is not there today, but the beggar is. And taking in money, too.

16. Mrs. Cowley.
17. Published originally in *PMLA* 84 (Jan. 1969): 136–37, with the kind permission of Miss Porter, Mr. Cowley, and the director of the Newberry Library, Mr. L. W. Towner; and with the generous help of Mrs. Amy Nyholm. Letter Copyright 1968 by Katherine Anne Porter.
18. P. 3.
19. The Modern Collection, Newberry Library, Chicago.

Chapter II

1. I prefer the term *novella* to *short novel* because it designates a different genre; I will go into the difference in my treatment of "Noon Wine."
2. *Harper's*, September 1965, pp. 59–68. The interviewer was Hank Lopez.
3. Note Miss Porter's classical terminology.
4. The fourth materialized as *Ship of Fools*.
5. In an interview in *Paris Review* (Winter–Spring, 1963), pp. 88–114, Miss Porter said she wrote "Flowering Judas" in five hours. She told me in Connecticut some years ago that "it fell off the typewriter."
6. Introduction to *Flowering Judas and Other Stories* (New York, Modern Library).
7. "The *Paris Review* Interviews," *Writers at Work*, 3d ser. (New York: Viking Press, Inc., 1967), pp. 251–78.
8. All references to Miss Porter's shorter works are from *The Collected Stories of Katherine Anne Porter* (New York: Harcourt, Brace & World, Inc., 1965), and page numbers are indicated in parentheses.
9. Listed erroneously in at least one published bibliography as having appeared first in 1938.

10. Leaf 10, as follows:

>She lives again who suffered life,
>She suffered death, and now set free
>A singing Angel, she forgets
>The grief of old mortality.

The phrase "old mortality" is from Scott. Miss Porter, presumably on the occasion when she gave the typescript to the University of Texas library, noted in her own hand to the right of these verses: "An original *pastiche*, not a quotation. K. A. P. Unrestricted use of this typescript is by courtesy of the University of Texas, and by kind permission of Miss Porter."

11. "Katherine Anne Porter: Irony with a Center," *Kenyon Review* 4, no. 1 (Winter 1942): 31.

12. "From the Notebooks of Katherine Anne Porter—Yeats, Joyce, Eliot, Pound," *Southern Review* 1, n.s., no. 3: 570–73.

13. "Faulkner's 'Sanctuary' and the Southern Myth," *Virginia Quarterly Review* 44, no. 3 (Summer 1968): 423–44.

14. "Interview with Katherine Anne Porter," in "The *Paris Review* Interviews," *Writers at Work*, 2d ser. (New York: Viking Press, Inc., 1967), pp. 89–90.

15. "Poetry, Language and the Condition of Man," *Centennial Review* (Winter 1960), pp. 1–15. This article appeared in two parts, the second written by Roy Harvey Pearce.

16. "Vitae nomen sumitur ex quodam exterius apparenti circa rem, quod est movere seipsum; non tamen est impositum hoc nomen ad hoc significandum, sed ad significandum substantiam, cui convenit secumdum suam naturam movere seipsam vel agere se quocumque modo ad operationem. et secumdum hoc vivere nihil aliud est quam esse in tali natura, et vita significat hoc ipsum, sed in abstracto, unde vivum non est praedicatum accidentale sed substantiale." PP. Q. 18. Art. 2 c.

[Now the same is to be said of life. The word is applied to things because of something in their external appearance, namely self-movement; nevertheless it is not applied to indicate precisely that, but rather the substance which of its nature has the power of moving itself or giving itself any kind of impulse to activity. In the latter sense "to live" means simply to exist in such a nature; and "life" means the same but in the abstract; just as "running" (the noun) means the act of running in the abstract. Hence "living" is not an accidental predicate but a substantial one.] Thomas Aquinas *Summa Theologiae*, trans. Thomas Gornall, S.J. (New

York and London: Blackfriars, McGraw-Hill, 1952), pp. 118–19.
17. Introduction to "Flowering Judas."
18. Miss Porter wrote to me on December 18, 1968: "Happy New Year if there can be such a Year While People rule the world!"
19. Morris L. Ernst, *The Best Is Yet* (New York, 1945), p. 118.
20. "The Eye of the Story," *Yale Review* 55, no. 2 (Winter 1966): 268–69.

Chapter III
1. George Core, who has written very perceptively of her work, recognized that "one of the most important technical aspects of Miss Porters' fiction and of fiction by and large still remains to be dealt with, and that is the problem of defining and understanding the form of the short novel. . . ." *Georgia Review,* 20, no. 3 (Fall 1966): 291.
2. Miss Porter wrote in "Three Statements about Writing," *The Days Before* (New York: Harcourt, Brace & World, Inc., 1952), p. 123: "The James-minded and the Whitman-minded people have both the right to their own kind of nourishment. For myself, I choose James, holding, as I do, with the conscious, disciplined artist, the serious expert against the expansive, indiscriminate 'cosmic' sort."
3. Howard Nemerov, "Composition and Fate in the Short Novel," *Graduate Journal* 5, no. 2 (Winter 1963): 375–91, did very brilliantly for the novella what Aristotle did for tragedy. His argument that this form is allegorical is convincing. One can imagine, for example, Mr. Thompson, among Dante's damned, as "This scum, who's never lived, now fled about, naked and goaded" (*Inferno,* trans. Sayers, canto 3).

Chapter IV
1. *Encounter* 14, no. 2 (February 1960): 70.
2. *Harper's,* September 1965, p. 67.
3. Louis Auchincloss, *Pioneers and Caretakers* (New York, 1965), pays some attention and much tribute to Miss Porter as a *woman* writer.
4. Lopez, *Harper's,* September 1965.
5. *Encounter* (February 1960).
6. Ibid.

7. D. H. Lawrence, *Lady Chatterley's Lover* (New York: Grove Press, Inc., 1957), pp. 273–74.
8. *The Deed of Life: The Novels and Tales of D. H. Lawrence* (Princeton University Press, 1963), pp. 16–17.

Chapter V
1. (New York: Farrar, Strauss and Giroux, 1969).
2. *The Days Before.*
3. See Harry John Mooney, Jr., *The Fiction and Criticism of Katherine Anne Porter* (University of Pittsburgh Press, 1962), and William L. Nance, *Katherine Anne Porter and the Art of Rejection* (The University of North Carolina Press, 1964).
4. *Virginia Quarterly Review* 36 (Autumn 1960): 598–613. Miss Porter wrote in "Flowering Judas," "The gluttonous bulk of Braggioni has [for Laura] become a symbol. . . ." A writer who would try to depend on symbols to illustrate the obscure would be unlikely to indulge in such explicitness.
5. See Dorothy S. Redden, " 'Flowering Judas': Two Voices," *Studies in Short Fiction* 6, no. 2 (Winter 1969): 194–204. A worthwhile stylistic analysis of the language of "Flowering Judas" by Beverly Gross, "The Poetic Narrative: a Reading of 'Flowering Judas,' " *Style* 2 (Spring 1968): 129–38, argues sensibly for the poetic quality of the work concluding, "The final point about its poetic language and form is that they are there to support the telling of a story."
6. *The Art of Modern Fiction* (New York: Rinehart, 1949), pp. 287–91. A lengthier version appeared in *Accent* 7 (Spring 1947): 182–87. It is interesting that what appeared in the earlier reading as "Obviously, a great many details have symbolic references, not the least of which is the title itself," had in the later reading been hardened into the dogmatic, "The first and most important symbol appears in the title itself: 'The [*sic*] Flowering Judas.' "
7. *Recent Southern Fiction: A Panel Discussion. Bulletin of Wesleyan College* 41, no. 1 (January 1961): 12. In the same discussion Miss Porter added, "Well and then another thing, everything can be used as a symbol. Take two of the most innocent and charming sounding, for example, just in western Christianity, let us say the dove and the rose. Well, the dove begins by being a symbol of sensuality, it is the bird of Venus, you know, and then

it goes on through the whole range of every kind of thing until it becomes the Holy Ghost. It's the same way with the rose which begins as a female sexual symbol and ends as the rose of fire in Highest Heaven. So you see the symbol would have the meaning of its context. I hope that makes sense."

8. West and Stallman, on the other hand, define "realism to contrast with symbolism. . . . The realistic level is the level upon which objective action takes place in close imitation of natural life." For them the symbolic does not seem to partake of the real.

9. Whit Burnett and B. C. Hoffman, eds., *This Is My Best* (New York: The Dial Press, 1942), pp. 539–40.

Chapter VI

1. *Collected Stories*, p. v.
2. See chap. 4 for Miss Porter's use of this image from her life.
3. See R. P. Warren, "Irony with a Center," p. 42.
4. James Joyce, *Dubliners* (New York: Viking Press, Inc., 1961), p. 100.

Chapter VII

1. Exceptions are George Hendrick, *Katherine Anne Porter* (New York: Twayne Publishers, Inc., 1965), and Harry John Mooney, *The Fiction and Criticism of Katherine Anne Porter* (University of Pittsburgh Press, 1962). In both studies "The Leaning Tower" is dealt with intelligently and respectfully, although Hendrick does not see the novella as thematically rich and Mooney's treatment is general.
2. *Katherine Anne Porter* (Universty of Minnesota Press, 1962).
3. *Katherine Anne Porter and the Art of Rejection* (University of North Carolina Press, 1964).
4. "Katherine Anne Porter: The Larger Plan," *Kenyon Review* 25 (1963): 671–95.
5. *Henry James* (University of Minnesota Press, 1963).

Index

114

M. M. Liberman is professor of English at Grinnell College, Grinnell, Iowa, and a former fellow of the Newberry Library. He received his B.A. from Lafayette College, 1943, and his M.A. from New York University, 1946.

This manuscript was edited by Marguerite C. Wallace. The book was designed by Mary Jowski. The type face for the text is Linotype Caledonia designed by W. A. Dwiggins in 1937; and the display face is Caslon Old Style designed by William Caslon in the 18th Century.

The text is printed on Warren's Olde Style paper and the book is bound in Columbia Mills' Bayside Linen and Vellum over binders' boards. Manufactured in the United States of America.